PEACE IN IRELAND

PEACE
IN
IRELAND

Two States, One People

DAVID BLEAKLEY

MOWBRAY

Mowbray
A Cassell imprint
Wellington House
125 Strand
London, WC2R 0BB

215 Park Avenue South
New York, NY 10003

First published 1995

British Library Cataloguing-in-Publication Data.

A catalogue record for this book is available from the British Library.

ISBN 0–264–67375–1

Printed and bound in Great Britain by Biddles Ltd, Guildford and King's Lynn

Contents

Preface

'The time for the healing of the wounds has come, the moment to bridge the chasms that divide us has come, the time to build is upon us.'
President Nelson Mandela, May 1994

THE IRELAND INTO WHICH I WAS BORN had been England's oldest colony for most of modern history; since 1169 it had been a long and often tragic colonial experience. Try as they might, the colonial rulers could not pacify Ireland, nor could they truly unite it. By the twentieth century the island, though deemed to be one administratively, was deeply divided. The colonial system could not endure.

After the First World War the British Government resorted to a desperate 'remedy' – partition. Political surgery was decided upon, severing North (six counties) from South (26 counties). The island was left almost fatally wounded; nor was there much aftercare, as the 'surgeons' hastily departed.

But the Irish are a resourceful people. Since partition, and notwithstanding fearful 'troubles' in both parts of Ireland (most recently in the North), there has been something of a miraculous recovery. Ironically, but steadily, in and through their separate jurisdictions, the people of Ireland for some seventy years have been moving towards an island-wide accommodation. Separate development has gone on, but there have also been significant moves towards non-threatening North–South co-operation, widely welcomed and increasingly encouraged.

This parallel movement, pragmatic in origin, is also the natural response of Irish people who feel urged to combine at many levels of shared needs and responsibilities. In effect a new polity of 'two states, one people' is being explored. It is an opportunity for shared enrichment which neither colonialism nor enforced territorial unity could have ensured.

As so often happens in real life, the power of people in Ireland is triumphing over defective political theories and the flawed political structures which they spawned. By trial and error and by dint of a setting-aside of many 'sacred cows' the Irish people are moving towards practical inter-relationships which attract island-wide support and offer parity of esteem to hitherto conflicting traditions.

The 'teasing-out' process will be demanding, but an all-Ireland will to succeed has emerged. Democratic forces in Irish society are reasserting their primacy as, increasingly, a modern population make clear their demand, ability and desire to live as equal citizens within separate jurisdictions. Equally insistent, the people of one island have begun collectively to appreciate the need and opportunity to join together as partners in custodianship for matters of common Irish concern. Hence the growing interest in an all-Ireland Bill of Rights.

So, North–South separation in citizenship is no longer seen as an insurmountable barrier to all-Irish progress. On the contrary, a proper use of what is on offer opens up attractive social and economic advances and provides a 'way into' real peace in Ireland. It is an idea whose time has come, and which is receiving island-wide endorsement.

In this setting, the Downing Street Declaration of December 1993 becomes the showcase for an historic break through in inter-Irish and Anglo-Irish relationships. But the essential promoters are the Irish people, North and South and of both main traditions, who separately and collectively are determining their own destiny.

Those in Ireland who have experienced the personal impact of shared 'defining moments' in our island's history are today part of the changing political atmosphere. We, too, are challenged to change – to accept a commitment to replace old fears and animosities by a climate of peace.

How we have arrived at this moment and where we go from here is what this book is about.

David Bleakley, 1995

PART ONE

A RADICAL PREPARATION

CHAPTER 1

Working-class Home

For me the journey into Irish peacemaking began in a working-class home in East Belfast in 1925. Here it was, near the shipyard gantries of Harland & Wolff, that my father, John Wesley Bleakley, a bricklayer from Co. Armagh, and his bride Sarah Wylie from Fermanagh, had set up home earlier in the century. They were part of the Victorian migration from the Ulster countryside which was to make Belfast one of the greatest industrial cities in Europe.

It was good to be born in Belfast. No mean city in 1925, it had been a pace-setter throughout the Industrial Revolution. Politically, too, it was a place with a radical past, having contributed to the Catholic Emancipation campaign as well as regularly commemorating the French Revolution and the fall of the Bastille. It was the sort of place where Tom Paine's *The Rights of Man* was widely discussed. All this was 'gospel', my father assured us, as he regaled the family with tales of our city's radical past.

For my father, a dedicated trade unionist, Belfast was special because of its contribution to the union movement. Proudly he reminded us that the earliest still-preserved trade union Minute Book is that of the Belfast Woodworkers Club, which held its first meeting in September, 1788, just in time to celebrate the forthcoming French Revolution. My father was also proud of the distinguished line of working-class leaders produced by the Province, among them John Doherty of Larne, described by Labour historian G. D. H. Cole as 'the most influential trade unionist of his time'; Bob Smillie, the noted Miners' leader from Belfast's Sandy Row; William Allen of Carrickfergus, first General Secretary of the Engineers. Irish names among the Chartists and other reform movements were legion – working people, we were reminded, had 'much to be proud of'.

From time to time, we were also referred to the family archives – recording the long links of the Bleakleys with the industrial facts of life.

I remember especially the Indenture of one of our forebears into the baking trade in nineteenth-century Co. Antrim. The rules were strict and bound the apprentice to 'faithfully keep his master's secrets, his lawful commands everywhere gladly do'. It was also laid down that the bound apprentice 'shall not commit fornication, or contract matrimony and he shall not play at cards, dice or any unlawful game. He shall not frequent taverns, ale houses or play-houses or absent himself from his said master's service day or night unlawfully'.

In return for all this the master pledged himself to 'find and provide during the said term of six years suitable diet and lodging, also one pair of boots in each year and pay him yearly the sum of one pound ten shillings'.

Such was the Indenture enforced in Victorian times. My father kept the document framed and hanging on the wall as a reminder to visitors that trade unionism was an essential fellowship for working people. 'Agitate, organize and educate' was his constant theme.

There was nothing fancy about our home, but we kept it spic-and-span: red cardinal on the tiled kitchen (the name in those days for the multi-purpose living room); the open fire, polished black and 'brassed' once a week; and a constantly whitened front doorstep for all our callers.

'Making-ends-meet crises' were regular. The golden rule was to avoid debt and as far as possible to share what we had with others.

Like many of my generation I recall the economic deprivation of the times. Bouts of unemployment for building workers were regular and we dreaded hearing that Dad had to 'go on tramp', looking for work in England or further afield. There was no alternative in the 1920s and 1930s when unemployment was widespread and state assistance meagre.

Even for those with steady jobs the rewards were small and working conditions often deplorable. In 1914, for instance, my father helped the carters who went on strike against a wage of eighteen shillings for a fifty-eight-hour week – and even they were not at the bottom of the industrial league. Many of our neighbours worked in the textile industry which was especially depressed. Inevitably it was the children who suffered most, dividing their day between work and school. These half-timers, some no more than eight years old, started work at six in the morning and after half a day in temperatures of over eighty degrees F. were sent off to school, covered in dust and moisture. Older members of the family talked much about their half-timer experiences.

The half-time system, which was not abolished until after the First World War, had a disastrous effect on the health of the children of Belfast. The mortality rate was higher than that of Manchester, which itself had a bad record. TB and rickets were feared by all.

In such circumstances working-class families were adept at making the household income stretch. We were brought up on well known 'make-things-go-further' rules: never two 'kitchen' (i.e. bacon *or* egg, not both);

soup made from the Sunday meat and served throughout the week; a 'sweet' only at weekends and special occasions; fruit rarely, and generally shared in half or quarter portions according to age. The darning basket was also an essential piece of household equipment, ready for repairs to socks and other pieces of clothing – 'a stitch in time saves nine' had meaning in those days! There was also a steel 'last' for do-it-yourself mending – the hammering home of steel protectors on heels and tips of new boots and shoes always preceded a first wearing.

When all else failed in the working-class economy there was always the pawn shop as a last resort. Many frowned on such transactions, regarding them as the beginning of a bad habit. But for others there was no alternative and the pawn shop, with its easily available loan on a personal or household possession, was a handy way to borrow a tiding-over payment. Housewives took charge of this business, with watches, musical instruments, clocks and Sunday clothes high on their 'pawning' list. Many a child of the time has memories of 'going a message' to the shop with its three brass balls sign – 'two to one you don't get it back' was the quip! The man of the working-class house was often unaware of the goings and comings of his household possessions. Little did he know that his 'Sunday best' was pledged during his working week. Woe betide the wife who failed to get the garment redeemed in time after pay day!

Other aids to balancing the budget were provided through the Penny Bank, the Co-op Quarterly Club and Christmas savings cards. Least popular of all were the local money lenders with their punitive rates of interest.

In such ways we helped one another in the Belfast of my boyhood. Long before state services intervened, the working-class devised its own central welfare system to reduce the grosser iniquities of poverty. Self-help was high on the list and the womenfolk, who often bore the brunt of the survival struggle, led the way. Working-class people in Belfast have fond memories of one such – Saidie Patterson, a pioneer union leader among women textile workers and a close friend of Transport and General Workers' leader, Ernest Bevin. Saidie understood her women members because she herself from childhood had been at the sharp end of domestic suffering. One story which Saidie told is a vivid reminder of that suffering. On 13 December 1918 the twelve-year-old Saidie was called to her mother's bedside. She had last seen her mother a few hours earlier as they had worked together on the latest batch of materials for the making-up factory (a childhood chore for many in textile Belfast). Saidie never forgot that bedside call and often thought about its full meaning:

> I remember that night as though it were yesterday. They brought me to my mother's room, just before she died in childbirth. She told me she was going to be with the Master we had often talked about,

and that I was to look after my new-born sister, Jean. 'You'll get help, Saidie, you'll get help'.

As I stood in my dear mother's blood, I didn't shed a tear, but I felt a cross being put on my back and, at the same time I felt a strange warmth coming into the room. Looking back now, I'm convinced it was the Holy Spirit.

From that day on I put my hand to doing what I could for what was right and the good Lord has honoured the bargain that was made at my mother's bedside. That night I became an adult.[1]

Saidie also became a socialist that night, determined to see that such things did not happen to other children. She was young at the time but she was haunted by the question, 'Why is it that my mother had to be cared for by a kindly but untrained local "handy woman" who was herself expecting a baby? And why was it that we weren't able to afford the three shillings and sixpence for a doctor?'[2]

Seeking the answer to questions like this made Saidie Patterson one of our leading social reformers. She became a role model to many young people in Northern Ireland. In our own household she was our elder 'sister' and godmother to our children.

Saidie Patterson taught us another important lesson about giving help – the need to carry out the service with sensitivity, so as not to give offence to those who might feel shamed by the suggestion of charity:

> You were always careful to be gracious in your giving. You pretended that you had made too much soup and wondered whether they would oblige by taking some of the surplus. You were also careful never to embarrass them by going to the front door – it was always the back entry you used. And when you were baking a griddle or two of bread you always put on extra farls to give to someone more in need than yourself. In that way we helped one another to get by.[3]

Much of this caring and sharing was directed through the local church, with tithing, a general guide to giving. For me the religious choice was wide – father was Church of Ireland and mother a Salvationist. So, from an early age I learned to be ecumenical; it was a case of observing Anglican order in St Patrick's, the 'Shipyard Church', on Sunday mornings, while in the evenings there was a chance to clap hands and sing songs to the accompaniment of tambourines and the Salvation Silver Band. 'Anglican Order and charismatic Joy' – not a bad mix I often thought.

Sunday, of course, was (and still is in much of Ireland) a special and different day. Church attendance was central to the Sabbath, with a real awareness that our presence was required. Not that we were especially holy, but rather that we saw religion as part of a normal human existence.

Indeed, those who didn't go to church were regarded as a bit unusual and even today in Ireland neglect of one's church is not regarded as something to boast about.

Sunday observance brought a good many rules to do with personal behaviour. Outdoor games were frowned upon in our locality and indoor activities were equally monitored. Even if you owned a 'pack', the 'Devil's cards' were never produced on the Sabbath. In our house we were pretty strict and for many years even the Sunday papers were regarded as doubtful reading. Later in the Stormont Parliament I had a Methodist colleague who preferred not to discuss business on the Lord's Day and was distinctly uneasy about accepting a trading cheque with a Sunday date.

But there was also a positive side to Sunday. It was a time of well-earned rest when people were glad to refresh mind and body and to get away from the weekday grind. It was also a chance to dress up and to enjoy one another's company in the church 'fashion parades', modest but socially meaningful, especially in the marriage stakes.

Like most modern urban communities the close comradeship produced by the shared struggles of earlier periods has been eroded, but in 1920s and 1930s Belfast the bond between neighbour and neighbour was strong – it had to be for survival.

Survival, of course, was not a problem confined to the Belfast working class; we were well aware of struggles on the Clyde and other shipyard areas. But whereas in Britain the political argument was largely class-centred, there was in Ireland an ever-present sectarian divide, cutting horizontally across society and weakening working-class unity when the struggle for social reforms required solidarity of action.

From an early age I began to realize that the social and economic arguments of my trade union father were often swept aside by the sectarian forces of unionism and nationalism which surrounded us. But my father had no doubts. For him it was a case of Protestant and Catholic workers alike being exploited by what he called 'Orange and Green Tories', operating a policy of 'divide and conquer'.

In such circumstances community development strategies got short shrift from establishment politicians who stigmatized bridgebuilding groups as being dangerously 'neither one nor the other' on the great political issues of the day; for such people there was to be little in the way of political success or preferment. This was to be the fate of the trade union and Labour movement with its long-standing tradition of non-sectarian politics.

The unsureness and violence of the 1920s encouraged tribalism in Ulster with each group, Protestant and Catholic alike, living ghetto-like existences, physically and mentally. The majority Unionist Party made use of this situation and where they had power discriminated on a religious basis against their opponents, particularly in the field of employment.

Where unemployment was concerned Protestant working-class suffering was also great. My bricklayer father was more often than not out of work in the years of the Depression, and as a family we often supported the out-door-relief (ODR) marches of the day. But Catholics in the immediate backlash of the 1920 (Partition) Act felt a special vulnerability, deserted by Dublin and unprotected by London. They realized that not all Protestants lived in the lap of luxury, but, as a republican-socialist MP once remarked to me, the Catholic working class felt that they were an especially depressed group within a depressed class.

But even in the early days of the Northern Ireland state there were those – albeit a radical minority – who did publicly promote peacemaking and sought for Protestant–Catholic unity. In our home, for example, we were always encouraged to seek a radical analysis to the social problems of the day and we learned to castigate preachers who turned religion into 'an opiate of the people'. Many of our connection got their spiritual guidance from Dr Arthur Agnew and his socialist Sunday School in Belfast's dock area. From regular visitors to our East Belfast house I heard much about the 'greats' of the Labour movement. William Walker, for instance, who in 1905, with Ramsey McDonald as his agent, stood as a parliamentary candidate for Labour in North Belfast and came within 510 votes of winning this Unionist stronghold. It was a famous almost-victory which has never been repeated.

Keir Hardie, MP, was a special hero in working-class folklore. As far back as 1893 he had formed one of the earliest Independent Labour Party branches in Belfast, not long after the first foundation in Britain. The blend of Christianity and socialism he offered was especially attractive in an Irish setting. A favourite text from Hardie for all of us was his Bible-based definition of Christian Socialism:

> Socialism is the return to that kindly phase of life in which there shall be no selfish lust for gold, with every man trampling down his neighbour in his mad rush to get most. What is now known as Socialism is woven from the same web as was the vision of Isaiah, and is also, without doubt, of the same texture as that Kingdom of God which the early Christians believed to be at hand.[4]

Here, indeed, was a view of life which offered an alternative to the strife of the times. I warmed to that definition and years later included it in my first Election Address.

We learned, too, of the work of James Connolly, with his mould-breaking analysis of Irish politics, *Labour in Irish History*. Described by Robert Lynd as 'Ireland's first socialist martyr', Connolly was executed in 1916 for his part in the Easter Rising. My father's comment was: 'They knew what they were doing when they got James Connolly. If he had lived, the revolution in the South might have amounted to something more than the greening of red Post Office boxes and the changing of street names from English to Irish'. He was making the point that 'revolutions' in Ireland were often pretty conservative in social and economic consequences. Later I was to read a more pungent and politically irreverent remark on the 'revolution' by Dominic Behan:

> The name plates on the streets were being changed into Irish, with the English of them underneath – otherwise how would folk know where they were going? 'Sraid Talbot – Talbot Street', 'Cul-de-Sac – Cul-de-Sac', Lord, isn't the Gaelic language wondrous beautiful? . . . Thank God the men of '16 have not given their lives in vain. Only one place had its old name: the Labour Exchange.[5]

As the passions of the 1920s revolution have faded, the Ulster people are learning to relax with one another and are certainly a much more tolerant people than their public and published image sometimes indicates. But growing up in a divided community is not easy. Tyrone Guthrie's comment rings true: 'So little that we manage to share in common – that's the tragedy of Ulster'.[6] This 'tragedy' expressed itself in some odd ways. For example, in childhood one became aware of a local code language that a stranger does not easily understand – using words in a way which reflects a religious or political affiliation. Indeed, sometimes the very pronunciation indicates a difference – try, for instance, to get a consensus on how to say 'H-Block'!

This code language is often used (and more so these days) in good part; but it still remains for many the way into the other person's 'tribal' grouping. A 'Patrick Malachy' will certainly indicate a Roman Catholic, just as surely as Robert John will be Protestant. The place of schooling, address, football scarf and the choice of which games to play or days to celebrate are all part of the identification process. Place names, too, cause trouble. For example, on the choice of name for 'Derry' or 'Londonderry' there has been much dispute. Significantly, however, it was a comedian who came up with the idea of 'Stroke City' – an ambiguity which brings a relieved smile and general acceptance.

There is, indeed, a welcome blurring of the more unhelpful of such distinctions. Young people, in particular, display a growing willingness to explore the two traditions and to share in a common culture. A vital factor in this coming together may prove to be the increase in the growth of inter-church marriages. A recent church report reveals that 'one in sixteen Northern Ireland marriages are mixed marriages; they have increased since the 1950s and are still rising'. Here the churches need to be sympathetic and supportive – and have been increasingly so in recent years.

In my boyhood days such ecumenism at the altar was a rare event and interchurch relations were at a low ebb, though there was always a courageous minority willing to reach beyond the divide. My father was one of these and taught us to get beyond sectarian explanations of the evils around us. Unemployment, for instance, we were encouraged to regard as a social defect and not, at heart, a matter of sectarian discrimination. Sectarianism could certainly add to social tension caused by unemployment, but the cure lay in matching job numbers and the labour demand. As he put it in Micawber-like language: 'Ten jobs, nine seekers – happiness; ten seekers, nine jobs – misery'. All good radical stuff, reinforced with guided reading in Blatchford's 'Merrie England' and other socialist classics.

Out of all this early preparation for peacemaking I value in particular the stress laid on reaching across the religious divide. It wasn't known as ecumenism in those days – it was just decent, sound common sense. But in Northern Ireland terms it was still considered future-tense thinking far ahead of its time. 'Religion is an accident of birth' we were taught, 'none of us picked our father and mother'.

The advice may have been homespun, but it was long-lasting in effect. Had it been applied more widely there would have been no '1969'. For me the abiding lesson in ecumenical behaviour came one day on returning from school after an R.E. lesson. I asked my father what was the difference between Protestants and Catholics. He thought for a moment and then he said: 'Do you know Paddy Falloon?' I did, indeed. Paddy and my father were bricklayers – two 'brickies' – who had knocked about for a lifetime looking for work for each other and working as partners. Paddy, a widower, was a regular and popular guest in our home, coming every Saturday in life for a meal with us, plying the children with gifts and amusing us with lively stories.

All this provided my father with the answer to my question – it was simple but memorable: 'Well, son, it's like this. You know Paddy Falloon who comes here every weekend – well, he's a good Catholic and all his family too. That's what Catholics are like and remember there's plenty more like Paddy all over Ireland. So whenever you think of a Catholic and what they're like, just you think of your friend, Paddy.'

That settled the matter for me, once and for all. Later on at impressive international gatherings I would probe the matter as part of a deeper intellectual exercise, but I was always building on the wise advice of my bricklayer father, based on real-life experience among his fellow countrymen in every Irish Province.

It was a guideline for life. If being a good Roman Catholic was being like Paddy Falloon and if being a good Protestant was being like my father, then I could respect and trust in the faith that produced such men. In their lives they told me more about belief and witness than any library could reveal. The absurdity of religious intolerance was obvious.

As Saidie Patterson said, bigotry did indeed go out with 'hobble skirts and button boots'.

This view of basic human values was underlined in the next stage of my journey into peacemaking – an apprenticeship in the shipyard of Harland & Wolff, one of Ulster's great industrial foundations.

REFERENCES AND NOTES

1   David Bleakley, *Saidie Patterson, Irish Peacemaker* (Blackstaff Press, 1980, p.12).
2   *Ibid.*
3   *Ibid.*, p.5.
4   *Ibid.*, p.46.
5   Edward Norman, *A History of Modern Ireland* (Penguin Books, 1973, p.289).
6   Bleakley, *Peace in Ulster* (Mowbray, 1972, p.47).

CHAPTER 2

Belfast Shipyard – A University of Life

W<small>HEN</small> I <small>TURNED</small> <small>FIFTEEN</small> my father said: 'It's time you got into a trade – why not try the Yard?'

For someone born and bred in East Belfast the shipyard of Harland & Wolff seemed the natural place to be. As children we had been brought up on the folklore of the yard, hearing tales about the early founders. We still heard of the international exploits of men like Lord Pirrie, acclaimed as Ireland's greatest industrialist and finest shipbuilder in the world. The names of our mightiest ships were known to all of us: Teutonic, Oceanic, Olympic, with the tragic Titanic still etched on all our memories.

So, getting into the shipyard was considered a fitting start to any work-ing life and especially the promise of a trade. Indeed, I remember the first time I was taken home by Winnie, my girlfriend, to meet her mother. After the usual introduction and inspection, that wise housewife con-cluded: 'Well, daughter, I'm glad to see he has got a trade; there's security in that'. Mrs Wason knew her facts of life: having a trade in those days was a considerable asset, offering a way into job security and a chance of promotion. Other much sought-after 'steady' jobs were in transport, Post Office, civil service and local government, but many of these were reserved for the grammar school educated or for those who had someone on the inside to 'speak' for them.

So, one December morning, in 1940, twelve of us turned up at the Queen's Road offices of Harland & Wolff to be 'indentured'. We were a pretty bewildered bunch as we experienced our first meeting with a ship-yard 'hat' – the name given to managers because of the black bowler hat they wore as a symbol of their authority. 'Watch out for the hat' we soon learned was the alert signal throughout the yard. Our 'hat' that morning was a no-nonsense manager who quickly put us through our paces and made it clear that we would be processed as he knew best. That meant being allocated a trade on a random basis. He hoped that we would be happy with the outcome, but there would be no room for 'chopping and changing'.

I had hoped to be a fitter or lathe turner, but when my turn came it was 'Bleakley – electrician' – or, more commonly, 'spark'. Industrial democracy and job selection procedures were a long way off in those days; but, in practice my 'take it or leave it' offer proved not a bad beginning. Certainly when they heard the news at home they were duly impressed. I noticed, however, that there was no great rush to take up my suggestion that soon I'd be able to wire up their gas-lit houses for electricity!

Inside a week I settled into the yard and began to learn its special geography, based on gantries, docks, workshops and drawing offices. Of great importance in getting around was the possession of the check-in identification number issued to all, and stamped on a small piece of wood which had to be collected each morning and returned to the time-office each night. The 'board', as it was called, was all important as a shipyard passport and you knew that you were in trouble when a 'hat' demanded its surrender. My own number was 25555, out of a vast community of more than thirty thousand workers. On a recent visit to Harland & Wolff I was told that there are now fewer than four thousand in the yard; I often wonder where the rest have gone.

I soon discovered that the shipyard was more than a place where ships were built. It was also a living community, catering for many human needs – a vast melting pot. In wartime Belfast the melting pot aspect was particularly significant. In the early and violent days of the Northern Ireland State there had been a cruel mass expulsion of Catholics from the yard, after which the labour force was sectarian in composition. The wartime shortage of labour brought a change. Even the occasional Catholic 'hat' was appointed, as the vastly augmented labour force became more inter-denominational and especially as Catholics from the South flocked North in search of wartime work. Many of these migrant workers brought families with them and so, as often happens, the demands of the industrial machine wrought changes for the better in employment patterns which sectarian employment strategies could not achieve. Shared pride in survival during German air-raids on Northern Ireland ('there are no orange or green bombs' as the phrase went) combined with fire fighting assistance from the South also promoted hands-across-the-border attitudes. Another bridge-building bonus was the common knowledge that Irish people, North and South, were flooding into the British armed forces and more than any other group in the Commonwealth had distinguished themselves in the collection of VCs and other decorations for gallantry. Important contact at the highest level was made between Irish and British comrades-in-arms. Indeed, at some of the most important 'Big Three' meetings half of Churchill's staff was Irish, while the list of great Commanders from Ireland was long: Alexander, Brooke, Cunningham, Dill, Montgomery, to name but a few. For most in Ireland there was no border in the struggle against Hitler and, in what was known as 'aggress-ive neutrality', the Irish served the allied cause at every level.

Timothy Patrick Coogan tells a whimsical story about the RAF which well sums up this aggressive neutrality:

> The navigator of a wholly Irish bombing crew in a plane buffeted by flak over Berlin is said to have muttered under his breath over the intercom as something nasty came through the fuselage 'Thank God de Valera kept us out of this'.[1]

All of Ireland enjoyed the story – one of many which were encouraging markers on the way to an easier North–South relationship. In such a changing climate it was a good time to be starting a shipyard apprenticeship.

As a new apprentice I was very much at the bottom of the shipyard pile and knew little of such goings-on. To start with, we had to go through the various initiation processes before being admitted to the senior pack. Newcomers were invariably sent to the storeroom for 'a bucket of blue steam', a 'sky-hook', a tin of 'striped paint' or some other mysterious, but non-existent, yard commodity. 'Try the store down the next wharf' was the advice given to hapless seekers, until at last there was a dawning of truth or the intervention of a sympathetic journeyman.

Depending on the skill and teaching patience of your allocated journey-man 'mate' the threads of shipyard duties were soon picked up. Before long I was clambering about the cranes fixing temporary lights or what-ever else required attention. Even more exciting was the occasional chance to get to sea on the trials of the destroyers or submarines which we built for the Battle of the Atlantic. The food on such outings was a great improvement on wartime rations and we enjoyed the comradeship of the naval crews as they tested out our workmanship.

Beyond this departmental framework the yard provided a whole world of non-work relationships. Meal hours and other breaks offered a market-place of choices, with a content and range sufficient for most needs. For those in search of simple relaxation there were games of skill: quoits, draughts and chess, along with the usual games of chance. Others would have none of these and organized Bible discussion groups in friendly but holy opposition. Radical politics was also on the menu. For those in search of instruction there was the chance to buy *Labour Weekly*, the more left-wing *Communist Daily Worker*, or the really trendy 'left' Trotskyist magazine *Socialist Appeal*. Followers of the faiths expounded on their political pamphlets.

Most literary of all were the groups centred on readings and discussions of magazines like *John O'London's Weekly*, *Strand Magazine*, *The Countryman* or Robert Lynd's latest essay in the *News Chronicle*. Sometimes the advice was more practical – like that from 'Buster' McShane and his keep-fit devotees who sought recruits for their body-building Health Studios which were soon to become all the rage. 'Buster', who died tragically early in life, did much to bring Ulster's young people together by offering them a physical culture outlet which was both ecumenical and personally beneficial. Buster McShane also became well known in worldwide sport through his management of Ulster's popular Olympic gold medallist, Mary Peters.

Hovering around this University of Life were the great characters of the shipyard – stimulating 'dons' giving a 'lift' to the proceedings with their witty opinions and often eccentric behaviour. Belfast shipyarders of the war years recall with affection their special favourites. Joe Tomelty, a painter by trade, who kept us all going with his ability to tell a good story and who went on to gain fame on radio, stage and screen. Another painter 'star' was Sam Thompson, whose prophetic play 'Over the Bridge' caused a sensation in its day because of its theme of sectarian shipyard violence; even the BBC hesitated to give it a slot, so great was the furore. Sam was also a splendid talker and at public meetings an expert handler of the constant interrupter. I remember one turbulent occasion when he stopped a female in her virago-like heckling tracks with the magnificent, but incomprehensible, remark: 'Madam, you are dancing about like a Bulgarian hemstitcher'. We all wondered what he meant; but it sounded so profound that it had the desired effect!

Another character from the yard who stood out in those days was gentle Tommy Carnduff. Known as the 'Shipyard Poet', Carnduff with his vivid word pictures of proletarian life among the gantries and slipways has done for Ulster's working class what Robert Service did with his tales and verse about workers in the Yukon.

Keeping this thriving community of shipyard people in order and giving leadership was the towering figure of Sir Frederick Rebbeck, shipbuilder extraordinary – or 'Lord Concrete', as he was affectionately known because of his constant pouring of new roads, buildings and docks into Europe's greatest yard.

But for the new apprentice the man who really counts is your first 'mate' – the journeyman with whom you will work and learn the trade. I was fortunate in my placement; I was assigned to Frank Gibson, one of the Electrician Union's best known shop stewards. Frank, a widely travelled and brilliant electrical engineer, was also an ardent internationalist. He had a special interest in Esperanto and like many of his associates believed that world peace would come if we all spoke a common language. Frank, like many men of his generation, was also a strong supporter of the USSR and before the crimes of Stalinism were revealed thought highly of Soviet achievements. Indeed, his first gift to me was a copy of the Dean of Canterbury's book 'Socialist Sixth of the World'. I had never heard of the 'Red Dean' and was surprised to learn that High Anglicans could be so left-wing in their social witness. Under the guidance of my mate I was to read many more of Victor Gollancz's Left Book Club publications. Reynold's *News on Sunday* was also required reading and a topic for discussion every Monday morning. Frank insisted that his apprentices should be well read!

Frank Gibson also introduced me to the Electrical Trades Union. I became a regular attender at the weekly meeting and soon its youngest officer as Minute Secretary. It was at these gatherings that the real learning about life in industry and politics was carried on. Meetings were carefully conducted and many a future MP or Councillor had a first training at the branch meeting. Chairmanship, in particular, was of a high order, led by officers who were as well read in Sir Walter Citrine's indispensable *ABC of Chairmanship* as was Parliament's Mr Speaker in his equivalent *Erskine May*. Certainly no one who has experienced life on the branch floor of an active trade union need ever fear parliamentary debate or boardroom discussion.

Behind much of this expertise lay the sound training provided by the trade union-funded National Council of Labour Colleges. Our ETU branch was affiliated, so members were entitled to use the network of lecture and postal course services operated from Tillicoultry in Scotland. Long before the Open University was created, the NCLC offered its wide range of postal courses for men and women countrywide and did much to discover and develop the intellectual potential of its working-class adherents. The impressive operation was presided over by J. P. M. Miller, one of the outstanding adult educationists of his day, and his dedicated and enthusiastic wife, Christine. Many MPs and other Labour leaders 'graduated' through the courses and have paid tribute to the pioneering work of the College movement. In my teens I too benefited, and especially from the tuition of its Irish organizer, Jack Dorricott, a former miner from Durham.

Trade Union education made me more aware of the social and economic ills of society and encouraged me to work for changes. As the War drew to a close, along with others of my generation I began to think of the brave new world we had all been promised; but I remembered, too, the comments of those who had come back after the 1914 War: 'They said in 1918 that they would build us a land fit for heroes. They did just that and it took you to be a hero to live in it!'

But Belfast in 1945 was an exciting and hopeful place in which to live. Winnie, my future wife, herself a shop steward in the clothing industry, and I decided to organize a youth section of the Labour Party. Along with our radical friend John Stewart, a young Methodist Minister from East Belfast, we decided to promote Christian Socialism as offering a way forward for Protestants and Catholics together. Heady stuff for twenty-year-olds, but shared by many in Ulster in 1945 who had experienced in war that there was another way of doing things; the pre-war world then seemed light years away. But how *did* one go about seeking the remedies for Northern Ireland; how did one get at the root causes pinpointed in the famous Beveridge Plan; how did one respond to the freedoms articulated in the Atlantic Charter? More study was indicated to bring some order into the chaos of casual reading in which we had become involved. But how?

As often happens, a way out appeared by chance. My journey into further education, a journey to Oxford, came early one Friday evening in January 1946 in, of all places, the local barber's shop. I had called in on my way home from work and, awaiting my turn, started to read a copy of *Picture Post*, a then famous illustrated weekly. An educational article caught my eye and before long I was completely absorbed. The heading was 'A Miner goes to Oxford' and it told the story of Ernie Fisher, who had gone to the University with the help of a TUC scholarship. Pictures showed him handing in his lamp for the last time at the pit-head and traced the story of his last days in the mining village to his first in Oxford. An interesting article, I thought, until an urgent nudge from my neighbour reminded me that I was still in the barber's and that it was my turn next. Very soon the clipping of scissors mingled with up-to-date gossip sent the article out of my mind.

But this story lingered on. I bought a copy of the *Picture Post* on my way home and read it again that weekend. Then came the thought, 'If a miner goes to Oxford why not an electrician? And why not me?'

'Yes, indeed, why not' was the comment of one of my older workmates when I raised the subject next day at break time. 'It may be a long shot' he said, 'but a twopence half-penny stamp will do more than all the talking in the world. Why not write off to Transport House and inquire?' With this sensible advice the subject changed and soon we were being treated to rival dissertations, this time on the value of education to the working classes!

Perhaps unconsciously I had been preparing for such a development. At that time I'd been working in the shipyard for about six years. The job was interesting enough and the pay sufficient, but like many an early school-leaver I had developed interests which full-time employment in the yard failed to satisfy. There were indeed the adult education classes of the Workers' Educational Association which Queen's University provided, and along with friends I attended these on a regular basis. But the 7.30–9.30 once a week occasions fell short of the in-depth study I sought.

So the possibility of a two-year residential course in such a college as Ruskin was attractive. The ethos of the College also appealed: a foundation for working men and women with a bias towards economics and other social science subjects. Also, as *Picture Post* indicated, Ruskin was unique among Oxford Colleges because of its close links with the trade union and Labour movement. Many Labour MPs and several Cabinet Ministers were among its graduates. It was, above all, a sound preparation for those who sought to change society along democratic socialist lines. Such information convinced me that Ruskin was my kind of College.

The next step was a letter to the Education Department of the Trade Union Congress, whose secretary informed me that four scholarships for Ruskin College and the London School of Economics were available for open competition among trade unionists in Britain and Ireland. Candidates were required to submit an essay to the TUC, after which short lists would be drawn up and interviews given. My subject was, and still is, a thorny one, 'A National Wages Policy', but it had to be tackled. With my shop-floor experience to guide me, I plagued the local librarian for books on the topic and eventually my research and reflections produced a two-thousand-word essay which I posted to Transport House along with a considerable application form, which asked penetrating questions about service in the trade union movement and local community associations.

After that things moved swiftly. I passed the first hurdle of shortlisting and was invited to London for interview. It was my first visit to Transport House, the Labour movement's holy of holies, and the pre-interview tour was an impressive start to the occasion. The panel was equally impressive, comprised of well known trade union General Secretaries, with Ebby Edwards, famous miners' leader, in the Chair. Also present were academics from Oxford and London colleges.

Some time was spent on my views on wages policy – here I had no trouble and my shipyard experience stood me in good stead. The real interest focused on what I had done with my time to date and in particular what sort of post-war future did I envisage. Some time was also given to the Irish situation, including the inevitable 'What about the Border?' question. Eventually came a summing up by Ebby Edwards and the last question: 'If you get this scholarship what would you hope to do afterwards?': 'Back to Ireland to serve the cause from Belfast' was the gist of my reply – at which the Oxford don (someone told me later it was A. J. P. Taylor) murmured, 'Mr Bleakley, you *do* recall that Gladstone's mission was to pacify Ireland and you know what happened to him!' Actually my knowledge of Gladstone was slight, but I had the wit to reply, 'I take the point'.

A few days later John Wray of the TUC's Education Department rang to say that all had gone well. I had been awarded a scholarship of £250 a year with £3 a week during vacations. After seven years with wires and switches and a sharing in shipyard fellowship I was turning to books and lectures for a while.

For me it was the chance of a lifetime which I have never regretted taking and have never undervalued. My Friday night visit to Billy Graham's barber shop had become for me one of life's defining moments.

REFERENCES AND NOTES

1   Timothy Patrick Coogan, *Ireland Since the Rising* (Pall Mall Press, 1966, p.89).

CHAPTER 3

Oxford Finishing School

'ARE YOU FOR RUSKIN?' – those were the first words I heard in Oxford one Saturday morning in October, 1946. They came from a fellow traveller on the Crewe/Oxford train. I had completed the journey from Belfast, having two days earlier checked in my shipyard 'board' for the last time. No longer No.25555, I was, with caution and considerable excitement, entering into a quite new world – and so was my companion.

My new acquaintance turned out to be Jack Ashley. It was a lucky meeting. He, too, was making for Ruskin College. Like me, he had come straight from industry – Widnes in Lancashire, where he had been a crane-driver. We had other things in common: working-class upbringing, trade union membership and an interest in Labour politics.

Jack thought that I was from Scotland. After leaving him in no doubt that Ireland was the address, we shook hands and decided to stick together at Oxford – we have been friends for a lifetime. Best man at my wedding, Jack got to know the Irish scene and has been sympathetic ever since. His wider sympathies with the disabled and other disadvantaged groups have earned him an international reputation. Various 'acts of defiance', as his biography calls them, illustrate what can be done when legislative power and a merciful heart combine. Later in life Jack and I each contested parliamentary seats and hoped to join up again on the floor of Westminster. 'Many are called, but few are chosen!' I regretted that I never managed to make the rendezvous.

Jack Ashley is an outstanding example of the enabling experience of a Ruskin College education. He is also a very good argument for the retention of the House of Lords, which he entered after a distinguished career in the Commons.

When Jack and I first met our initial task was to find Ruskin, which we did after a considerable walking tour of Oxford city. We agreed, as we looked around, that neither Widnes nor Belfast were anything like this. None of the calling horns of industrial life which punctuated each day back home – instead, the sound of ringing bells which had ordered College life for centuries. The scars of our industrial environments gave way to medieval stonework laid down by generations of unhurried craftsmen. How my bricklayer father would admire their skill, I thought on that first introduction to Oxford's cobbled streets and medieval buildings. Years later we recalled this Oxford meeting on TV's 'This is Your Life' tribute to Jack – and so our first impressions of university life were shared with a wider constituency.

The College, which was to be my home for two years, was founded in 1899 as a place where working men and women might enjoy the advantages of university life – a revolutionary idea in those days. John Ruskin had no direct connection with the College except insofar as it was named in honour of his progressive ideas. The founders were Walter Vrooman and Charles Beard, two distinguished Americans. They wanted a university centre for working-class students who would come to Oxford seeking not 'pounds and pence but a broadened and deepened life'. Or, as new students were reminded by the vice-principal, Henry Smith, 'your mission at Ruskin is to learn about the world so that you might change it for the better'.

There were many in Victorian Oxford who scoffed at the idealism of the pioneers, but with trade union and adult education support a successful founding was made. The College had grown into the famous education centre which greeted me on that Saturday afternoon in 1946. There were about a hundred of us at the first meeting: miners from Scotland and Wales; Manchester engineers; a quota of Yorkshire foundrymen and steelworkers. Nurses, typists, bakers, journalists and printers added to the occupational mixture. We were also international in texture and at our first meeting voices from places as far away as America, the West Indies, and several parts of Africa mingled with those from every region in Britain and Ireland. It was a stimulating mixture.

Some at that first meeting made an instant impression. David Edgar with his deep love of the countryside and later to figure as a distinguished agricultural journalist; Fred Riddell, already politically active, who became a formidable national leader in local authority education; gentle Saki Stevens, who would return to Africa to lead his country, Sierra Leone; and Joan Wicken, scholar and visionary, who post-Ruskin would join Julius Nyerere in a lifetime of service to the development of Tanzania, with its unique form of African family socialism.

But whatever our background we all received the same reminder of what Ruskin College was all about from Lionel Elvin, our distinguished Principal. He left us in no doubt that Ruskin was special. As he put it:

The hardest thing for a student at Ruskin is to achieve a synthesis between his life as a student and his experience as a worker; but if this is achieved the apparent withdrawal should make the return strong with renewed strength. In some ways such a period of study may seem to be a break. It is really a bridge, a bridge between the world of learning and the world of working life. To be such a bridge, to the enrichment of both worlds, is our perhaps not unambitious aim and has been our aim since the College was founded in Oxford with the support of British workers nearly fifty years ago.[1]

This was exactly in line with my expectations: we had been made aware of our opportunities and obligations right from the start. For myself, I could hardly believe my good fortune. Grant-aided to read, write, think and enjoy the society that is Oxford! 'How, compared with industrial life, can they call this work?' I thought, as we were launched on our course of studies.

The late 1940s was an exciting time to be in Oxford. In the immediate post-war years it was filled with students of my own age whose desire for higher education had been both interrupted and stimulated by the war. Future 'names' were generously sprinkled around the Colleges: Margaret Thatcher (née Roberts), Tony Benn, Robert Runcie, Kenneth Tynan and Ludovic Kennedy, to name but a few. Ruskin, too, had its prospective panel of 'futures': MPs and Cabinet Ministers galore, trade union leaders, industrial relations professors, high-ranking African leaders, including a future Prime Minister of Sierra Leone.

Anxious as we were to get down to the books and catch up on the lost years of the war, there was a still 'rich-beyond-the-college' Oxford to explore. Everyone, poet, politician or preacher was catered for. Ruskinites majored in many of the best debating encounters at the Oxford Union and our own College Hall. One term's selection included personalities as diverse as (Professor) C. E. M. Joad, Harold Laski, Professor Bernal, Anthony Eden, Clement Attlee. During my time as student Chairman of the College I had the opportunity to make contact with many whose fame I had known of only through their books. On one occasion I even had to contact George Bernard Shaw on behalf of our student body. Being a fellow Irishman carried no weight whatsoever! All I received was one of his famous 'no can do' postcards with his spidery writing and radically coloured ink.

A special encounter which meant much to me then, and more so in later years, was with one of Ulster's most famous literary sons. Ordering a coffee one morning in the popular 'Cadena' student café in Oxford's Cornmarket, I was interrupted by someone putting a hand on my shoulder and saying, 'What part of Belfast gave you that accent?' Looking up I saw a farmer-like man in sports coat and 'cords', who asked the question in what was clearly an Ulster accent. I told him my address and immediately he said, 'That's not far from where I live'. He was very interested to learn of my shipyard-to-university translation and before he left suggested that I might drop in to see him sometime in the College where he worked. 'Magdalen' he said, 'though these odd English pronounce it "Maudlin"'. He continued, 'Just call in at the gate-lodge and ask for C. S. Lewis.' The name rang a bell, but not very loudly. Later that night at dinner Lionel Elvin, himself an English Literature scholar, put me right: 'David, my dear fellow, that's one of Oxford's most interesting men; do go and see him'. And that was my introduction to C. S. Lewis.

We met from time to time (sometimes with Kenneth Tynan, one of his students). C. S. was easy to talk to and I was privileged to experience the skill of a great communicator, who got at the spiritual heart of things in language simple but memorable: 'If you cannot put your faith in the vernacular then either you don't know it or you don't believe it.'

Lewis was known to his close friends as an active and lively man who loved to walk and talk, expanding on his ideas as he went along. For those who were students he also shared his energetic outings. Sometimes he could be puckish. Walking together up Headington Hill one evening this great lover of both Oxford and the Co. Down, turned to me, feigning a need for advice: 'David, could you define Heaven for me?' I tried – he soon interrupted my theological meanderings: 'My friend, you're far too complicated; an honest Ulsterman should know better. Heaven is Oxford lifted and placed in the middle of the Co. Down.'

Not bad, not bad indeed. I am sorry that I was not then better prepared to appreciate this true son of my native county, but ever since I have become aware of how much C. S. Lewis 'country' we have to explore in Northern Ireland. Lewis left an enduring and much appreciated mark on all who knew him and I was no exception. Years later I felt a fellow feeling when Simon Barrington-Ward, Bishop of Coventry, shared with me the joy he felt on discovering that he, Simon, had been given a mention in one of his hero's books.

C. S. Lewis was one of the great teachers in post-war Oxford. There were others to whom I turned as special mentors. My chosen field was Politics, Philosophy and Economics, around which in Belfast I had engaged in a good deal of chaotic and largely unguided reading. Now, under the instruction of superb teachers, I had an opportunity to enlarge my range and get my material into some kind of order. For adult students, straight from industry and self-taught patterns, it was not easy to unlearn old habits and master university patterns. Like a new language, it took a bit of getting used to.

I was blessed with patient scholars who helped me put the pieces together. Chief of these were G. D. H. Cole, Professor of Political Theory, and Sir Hubert Henderson, Professor of Economics. My debt to these two men is immense. They gave me a grasp of core subjects and an overview of history and contemporary economics which helped make sense of questions which had arisen time and again in my preparatory industrial experience. G. D. H. Cole, in particular, who had a special affinity with Ruskin students, helped me greatly with his guided reading programmes. He also encouraged me to develop a Labour history interest; when I returned to Ireland in my subsequent work in industrial studies, he gave generous advice from his own research files. After two years with these scholars I began to feel something of an order which had been lacking in earlier self-help endeavours.

But neither Cole nor Henderson was giving me the linkage I sought between society and religion. All my upbringing and all my instincts suggested to me that there must be a linkage. Keir Hardie's Isaiah vision hanging on our kitchen wall in Belfast was not forgotten. Again provision came from Oxford. Around this time I had learned from a chance remark by C. S. Lewis that there was a special place of contemplation in Oxford, run by the Society of St John the Evangelist. He spoke highly of their work and witness in Oxford and further afield. They were Anglicans.

I decided to make my own contact and one night turned up for Evensong at the Society's monastery (they preferred to call it 'Mission House') at 16 Marston Street. There I met the Guest Master, Christopher Bryant, one of the Society's greatest thinkers – it was to mean for me a lifelong association and an opening of fellowship within the wider national and international Church.

The Society of St John the Evangelist (often called the Cowley Fathers because of its place of origin) was founded at Oxford in 1886 by Father Richard Benson – and it was the first religious community for men to be established in the Church of England since the Reformation. The foundation standards were high and have been well maintained. The aim was that the whole of life should be orientated towards God, always bearing in mind the changing conditions and demands of a rapidly changing world. In practical terms, today, that means open and well-ordered worship, links with education, arts and science; social outreach and personal counselling services.

Father Bryant was someone to whom we could all relate. Like many who had endured the horrors of war he had come to believe that it was not enough to rely on earthly experiences, however deep; we were required to engage from time to time in spiritual fine-tuning. This meant breaking the spell of earthly inertia and entering into the exploration of that for which we were created. He put it like this:

> Man is at present only half alive, he is imperfectly human, he is as yet *in the making*. God destines him to become human through and through, to become fully and abundantly alive in the land where, in

the company of his fellows, he will explore without end the unfathomable mystery of the Godhead.[2]

This to many of us looking for post-war personal guidelines was challenging stuff, confronting us with great 'What's it all about?' questions which tug at every soul and which came up persistently at our Ruskin College discussion groups when we tried to make sense of the world.

For me there was no doubt; these monks had an approach to religion and a lifestyle that made sense of a muddled world. Since then, as a member of the supporting Fellowship of St. John (FSJ), I have been deeply involved in the affairs of the Society and am one of its Trustees. The Society has been generous in its support for peacemaking in Ireland and for my international work as President of the Church Missionary Society. In addition, their House has been made available as an invaluable 'post-box' for many matters of Church and State. I owe them much. With some 300 men and women of the Fellowship, we accept the Society's guidelines for Community worship and witness. As members, we are encouraged to treat possessions as a trust from God and to practice moderation in eating and drinking. In addition, avoidance of excessive expense on dress and amusements is regarded as an opportunity for self-discipline in daily life and witness.

'A tough regime' the world might say. But not really – in everyday life benchmarks are helpful guides to action. Indeed, most monastic rules are little more than formal language for pretty sensible patterns of behaviour which make life more manageable and, above all, more meaningful. Personally, as an active peacemaker, I value and benefit from the constant concern and support of SSJE. So in Ireland when we try to follow the fourfold rule to pray peace, to think peace, to speak peace and to act peace I know that we have a link with the Society of St John as part of a wider circle held together in a fellowship of reconciliation.

But for many people monastic life is all a bit of a mystery, and the popular image of monks is largely a caricature. Most people still wonder what goes on behind monastery and convent walls. Indeed sometimes the media and the world at large seem to watch in fascinated anticipation for someone to 'leap over the wall' and tell what it's all about. I often wonder that they expect to find; my own experience is of men and women reflecting life in all its rich variety. And like the rest of us, with God's help, they get on with the business of coping with their daily 'ups and downs'. Nor are the monks short on knowledge of the world. On the contrary, I have been struck by the considerable pre-ordination experience in every walk of life of those in full communion. Indeed, some of the most significant peace initiatives in Ireland have been developed in monastic settings. I think of the remarkable long-term peace work engaged in by centres like Corrymeela, Columbanus Community, Servite Priory, Christian Renewal

Centre Rostrevor, Clonard Monastery Belfast – just a few in the countrywide network serving peace in Ireland. International mediators have also praised the facilitating work of such institutions. The great success of Dr Eberhard Spiecker, for example, in his work on behalf of the German Churches – the Duisburg peace process – has been continued for the past twenty years based on networking support from many in religious orders.

Coming, as I did from the County Down, I was well placed to appreciate Oxford's Cowley Fathers. From my town of Bangor, the tramp of Irish monks has been heard across Europe for 1500 years – France, Germany, Switzerland, Austria, Italy and even further afield; their presence was felt as they came not to colonize but to save. Cardinal Tómas O'Fiaich used to refer to Columbanus as 'the first European' – a contemporary recognition that monasticism has for long sought a balance behind and beyond the cloister.

One other debt I owe the Cowley Fathers – Christopher Bryant advised me to study the work of William Temple. It was good advice and like many of the laity of my generation I found in Temple's *Christianity and the Social Order* one of the most persuasive and lucid statements of the Church's attitude to the social system ever written. Here was an Anglican who was affirming 'the right and duty of the Church to declare its judgement upon social facts and social movements and to lay down principles which should govern the ordering of society'. And as an Ulsterman I was particularly pleased to note that Bishop George Bell of Chichester, whose mother came from Co. Tyrone, was a close ally of Temple and, like the Archbishop, was a thorn in the flesh of the Establishment – further reminders of Anglicanism's socially radical tradition.

Such intimations of Christian socialism were later confirmed in meetings with A. D. Lindsay, Donald Soper and George Macleod of Iona, all of whom encouraged me to promote the cause in Ireland. The promotion has continued ever since, though at times I found that seeds nurtured at Ruskin were being sown on less receptive soil. But ten thousand difficulties make not a doubt. As I wrote on my return in 1948: 'Socialism has a message for Christians everywhere, but for those who live in Northern Ireland it has a special message.'[3] The spelling out of that message would be the work of a lifetime.

Before I left Oxford one more important seed was nurtured – the seed of pacifism. Already in Belfast my father in supporting the Peace Pledge Union had made me aware that options other than violence were available for the solution of conflict. Was a non-violent strategy the missing factor in Ireland's search for peace, I often wondered.

A reading at Oxford of Gandhi's *Life and Ideas* brought home the universality of the pacifist appeal. It was one to which I could relate:

> I swear by non-violence because I know that it alone conduces to the
> highest good of mankind, not merely in the next world, but in this

also. I object to violence because, when it appears to do good, the good is only temporary, the evil it does is permanent.[4]

I also took great encouragement from Gandhi's trust in 'People Power' – another unharnessed force in Ireland in the 1940s, but one I sensed was there:

> It is said that non-violence cannot be attained by the mass of the people. And yet, we find the general work of mankind is being carried on from day to day by the mass of the people acting in harmony, as if by instinct. If they were instinctively violent, the world would end in no time. They remain peaceful. It is when the mass mind is unnaturally influenced by wicked men that the mass of mankind commit violence. But they forget it as quickly as they commit it because they return to their peaceful nature immediately the evil influence of the directing mind has been removed.[5]

Attendance at meetings in Oxford and London to hear George Macleod, Stafford Cripps and Pastor Niemöller confirmed my burgeoning belief that reconciliation must be centred in methods that were non-violent. Before returning to Ireland I made a commitment to work for peace at home and overseas through the Fellowship of Reconciliation. Subsequent experience in Ireland, and particularly the lessons learned in the 'troubles' following 1969, were to confirm this belief. Gandhi's faith in the power of the people to change society through non-violence was also confirmed on Irish soil. Paramilitary violence has been unable to win the battle that really mattered – that for the hearts and minds of the Irish people.

In the last months of my stay in Oxford I met a group of members of the Fellowship of Reconciliation and attended their weekend seminars. They impressed me as a company of Christians who had made a personal and binding commitment to peacemaking. Their worldwide Fellowship began in 1914 when, on the eve of the Great War and with the words 'We are one in Christ and can never be at war', a German Lutheran and a British Quaker, Friedrich Siegmund-Schultze and Henry Hodgkin, shook hands as they parted on Cologne station. Out of their initiative and after further discussions in England, about 130 Christians of many denominations met in conference in Cambridge towards the end of that year. After several days' discussion they decided to form a continuing society to be known as the Fellowship of Reconciliation.

Today the Fellowship of Reconciliation is a worldwide association of Christians of many denominations, and of none, who share the belief that justice cannot be founded on violence and that we must therefore try to meet violence, whether personal, national or international, with love. So it becomes incumbent upon those who believe in this principle to accept it fully, both for themselves and in relation to others and to take the risks in doing so in a world which does not as yet accept it.

In the Oxford of 1948 I had no difficulty in accepting such principles. They provided the extra dimension of peacemaking to Christian witness which so much of traditional theology, and particularly in Ireland, seemed to lack. Many decades later I am no less certain of the need for Christians to be so committed. But today there *is* a difference: whereas in 1948 I was a pacifist largely by *conviction*, now, in 1995, after a lifetime in the Irish peace movement, I have become a pacifist whose faith has been confirmed by the all-important test of experience.

Through FOR I have enjoyed a lifetime of fellowship with pacifists worldwide. I also had for some years the unique opportunity to work as a Visiting Senior Lecturer in Peace Studies at Bradford University. My colleague in this work was Brigadier Michael Harbottle, famous for his Blue Beret service in the Middle East and more recently for his development of the revolutionary (particularly to the military mind!) theory of 'Proper Soldiering'. With their stress on the use of the skilled energies of the military machine as servants for relieving human suffering, Michael Harbottle and his colleagues really are turning spears into pruning hooks.[6]

The Fellowship also provided an opportunity to get to know and work more closely with Martin Niemöller, who during the war became one of the greatest and most prayed-for names in Christendom. For those of us who were young in the 1940s Pastor Niemöller was a hero and inspirer. In his later years he gave invaluable assistance to the peace movement in Britain and Ireland. Together with John Prescott of the Church of Scotland we formed the international reconciliation group Christians Understanding Everywhere (CUE) which for many years has linked peace groups in Ireland, Britain, the Netherlands and Germany in work and study projects.[7]

I still keep on my desk a message sent by Niemöller to encourage me during a time of difficult decision-taking in Ireland: 'To be a Christian means to walk and live in the footsteps of our Master. That is Christian unity, that is faith, that is salvation. In this happiness, dear Mr Bleakley, I am your friend, fellow and brother.' (Martin Niemöller, Geneva, 20 July 1966.)

In all these ways Oxford became for me a finishing school, in preparation for work in Ireland which I had discussed at my scholarship interview with the TUC in 1946. Now in June 1948 all that needed to be addressed was the final academic reckoning when at the Examination Schools in Oxford's 'High' the result of all our study was to be tested. Here we were all equal. At one desk sat a Peer's son, at another a printer's. A few yards away my friend, Bert, from Jamaica struggled with the same questions as did I. In five days it was all over. After that a period of waiting – the results, the Diploma awards and then the sudden realization that our stay together was soon to end. The tension of pending examinations had obscured this reality and before we knew it we were caught up in the flurry of packing and beginning to think 'what comes next?' – a problem for all who graduate, but particularly so for adults for whom the post-graduate pattern was, in those more inflexible days, much less certain and more uprooting.

Among the men many returned to home-base. Tom to guide the Seamen's Union, Jock to the coal-mine, David to his farming and Eric to be a mainstay of adult education in Southwest England – our black friends to far-off homes and leadership responsibilities. Most of our women colleagues seemed more certain about their futures: Betty (later to become Baroness Lockwood) to raise the awareness of Labour headquarters and a wider constituency about the rights and potential of women; Joan to the manse to serve her Methodist Church; and Wyn, most radical of our females, to enrich the community with a life in social service, along with Jimmy, an American Ruskinite whom she had married. We were all settling into new lives.

For me, too, the wheel had turned full circle. In a few weeks I was back again in Belfast with Winnie, now my wife, and sharing plans for the radical future we foresaw. I was among my industrial friends again, for a while doing my old job, tussling with wires in an effort to bring light to darkened buildings. As we worked we sometimes talked of the journey I had made, of the people I had met, of the things we had done together. To them it seemed a long journey, but to me it had been all too brief. But brief or long, in the title words of one of C. S. Lewis's books which he was yet to write, I, too, at Oxford had been 'Surprised by Joy'.

The finishing school had had its effect.

REFERENCES AND NOTES

1   Lionel Elvin, *Ruskin Review* (New Epoch, Oxford, 1947, p.16).
2   Christopher Bryant, *The Heart in Pilgrimage* (Darton, Longman and Todd, 1980, p.181).
3   David Bleakley, *Christians and Socialism* (Ulidian Magazine, Queen's University Belfast, 1949).
4   Louis Fischer (ed.), *The Essential Gandhi* (George Allen and Unwin, 1963, p.201).
5   *Ibid.*, p.202.
6   See publications of Centre for International Peacebuilding and especially Michael Harbottle, *What is Proper Soldiering?* (Centre Publications, Chipping Norton, 1992).
7   See Brian Frost, *The Politics of Peace* (Darton, Longman and Todd, 1991, especially ch.8).

PART **TWO**

NORTHERN IRELAND – CRADLED IN PARTITION

CHAPTER 4

Government of Ireland Act 1920
– Partition: a Last Resort

In IRELAND ancient memories all too often take precedence over the affairs of the living. Season by sacred season, and with desperate earnestness, the command to celebrate and commemorate goes forth North and South. Many keep their heads down and wait for the various 'mad months' to pass, but courageous is the public figure who dares to 'step out of line'. In the South, more homogeneous in culture and religion, celebratory occasions in recent decades have become less politically volatile. The faithful still assemble to berate the ancient English enemy and to relive old wrongs, but in the main their demonstrations have as much impact on the nation's consciousness as has a colourful English miners' rally harking back to the Tolpuddle Martyrs. Affection certainly, but no real public involvement.

But in late twentieth-century Northern Ireland old memories linger on and it is all to easy to arouse fears and animosities which destroy a climate of peace. It is difficult to avoid the signs in Northern Ireland which enjoin the passerby to support the cause. Even the walls shriek their message: 'Remember 1690' say countless gable murals portraying William III and his white charger crossing the Boyne in the seventeenth-century Glorious Revolution cause. For those whose Protestant-loyalist history is more contemporary in remembrance there are plenty of recently painted 'Ulster Says No' signs, execrating the most recent constitutional landmarks. The Anglo-Irish Agreement of 1985 and the Downing Street Declaration of 1993 get special mention.

Catholic–republican appeals to the eye and emotions are equally colourful and emotional in their intent: Wolff Tone, Padric Pearce and James

Connolly are painted in on behalf of many a convoluted appeal. So, many an honourable slogan from a very different past is given a present-day nuance far removed from the intention of its originator. Like their loyalist counterparts, republicans are well supplied with tribal reminders: 'You are now entering Free Derry', 'A Nation once Again', 'Brits Out', 'Remember 1916'.

In such circumstances it is not surprising that the road to peace has been long and frustrating. It could hardly be otherwise, punctuated as Anglo-Irish history is with hesitation and fits of impatience. Since 1169 the flaws in the relationship between Ireland and Britain (essentially England) have been many and at times massive, resulting in one of history's great love–hate relationships. But behind the tension has remained a recognition that all of Britain and both parts of Ireland constitute a pattern of islands to which all sides belong – the 'Iona' (Islands of the North Atlantic) vision, as it is sometimes called, by those who proclaim it most vigorously.

Those who down the centuries have sensed such possibilities for creative integration have had to contend with formidable counter-forces. For example, the tension of being destined to be neighbours yet at the same time strangely distant. Henry Grattan's observation about Ireland and England over two hundred years ago still applies: 'Near enough to enforce connection; yet far enough away to discourage intimacy'. So, at regular intervals, and all too often as an exercise in crisis management, English and Irish together have been forced to the conference table to reconsider the association.

Until relatively recently inter-island discussions represented a confrontation between victor and vanquished, but in the third quarter of the twentieth century an historic sea-change has taken place – the conference table is at last round in spirit and parity of esteem (and personal trust and respect) between London and Dublin.

Still to be given adequate recognition is the need to admit Belfast as an equal partner to the conference table. This would recognize a new element in Irish public discussions – the coalition of Northern people, Protestant and Catholic together who, post-1969, have been emerging as one people, with a common consciousness. As yet, this consciousness is not fully articulated, but it is there to stay. Put bluntly, this means that in the final analysis there are limits to what London and Dublin can do to order North Irish affairs. They may propose – but they cannot impose. Indeed it would be the greatest irony of Irish history if the Republic, having got release from colonialism for its own twenty-six counties, were to aid and abet a political process attempting to impose colonial status on the Northern six counties with their own emerging and – in Anglo-Irish terms – complementary polity.

What is now needed is the creation of an agreed framework of constitutional arrangements which will give expression to such realities, be they inter-Ulster, inter-Irish or Anglo-Irish.[1]

Past history offers little consolation. Constitution-building has all too often left Ireland with a fresh legacy of recrimination. Unlike in England, there has been no island-wide Magna Carta by which the Irish people collectively could be assembled to mount a common defence of personal and political liberty. Certainly, the great pieces of legislation in Ireland may have constituted defining moments, but they were 'moments' which drove further communal wedges into an already divided populace. Such a moment came with devastating consequences in 1920 with the passing of the Government of Ireland Act – the Partition Act, as many called it.

The 1920 Act sought, through partition, to solve both the Ulster problem and the wider Anglo-Irish problem. Partition was not a new idea. It became more openly discussed in the Home Rule crisis of the later decades of the nineteenth century, when Gladstone's Home Rule Bill of 1886 greatly concentrated the minds of Ulster Protestants and produced a unity of purpose among them which was to bear down on the great statesman every time he took an initiative to fulfil his lifelong mission 'to pacify Ireland'.

As Ulster historian A. T. Q. Stewart reminds us in *The Narrow Ground*, what was publicly made clear between 1886 and 1920 was that Ulster Protestants felt themselves a minority under threat. So the history of Ireland in that period is shaped by their absolute determination not to become a minority in an independent, or even semi-independent, Catholic state. The 'Orange Card' to be played was time and again placed on the political gaming table to the discomfiture of the Liberal Prime Minister.[2]

However, the Northern 'difference' did not originate with Gladstone. Earlier observers had noticed it: 'The six northern counties of Ireland are so very differently circumstanced from the rest, that they very well deserve a separate consideration, if there be really any intentions of restoring the tranquillity of the country'.[3] A speech in favour of the 1920 Act or the 1993 Downing Street Declaration? Not a bit of it: as Stewart points out these were the sentiments of an 'Irish country gentleman' published shortly after the 1798 rebellion and serving 'as a salutary reminder that the idea of partition was not new in 1920'.[4]

What *was* new in the 1920s, of course, was the realization of what had happened: a distant threat had become a present reality. What could not be seen at the time, experienced by many as 'peace by ordeal', was the way in which partition once underwritten by powerful social and economic institutions might provide the basis for a new Ireland, divided but sharing a unity deeper than any possible in an enforced union. A generation of later revisionist Irish writers in the 1950s, notably Michael Sheehy and

John J. Horgan in *Divided We Stand*, began a challenge to traditional and restrictive views of Irish history.

But for Irish people in 1920 the need for such pragmatism was not yet apparent – partition had yet to be tried, largely through a reluctant process of trial and error. For the North, in particular, less so for the Republic and Britain, the price to be paid was daunting. Certainly the follow-up legislation of the 1920s eventually eased Anglo-Irish tensions on the British mainland and in the twenty-six counties of the Republic, but for the North the initial consequences were nothing short of calamitous as the unresolved issues of 750 years of colonialism were concentrated into the confined area of Northern Ireland. So, Ulster people, Protestant and Catholic together, had imposed upon them a virtually impossible agenda which they were left to get on with as best they could. London and Dublin governments looked to their own domestic concerns, each hoping that the 'Ulster problem' would go away. But it did not go away – after fifty years it engulfed the Ulster people in a hurricane of history which they could not control or fully understand. The unfinished business of 1920 was up for debate once again. Ulster's leaders would be asked to account for their stewardship. Equally, Dublin and London governments would be challenged to reassess the price that they would be prepared to pay for peace in Northern Ireland.

The choice presented to Northern Ireland in 1921 seemed to most a Hobson's choice. It was also the offer of a bewildered administration. Britain was exhausted after the First World War and Southern Ireland, also drained by that event, was bearing the additional cost of widespread civil war. Additionally Lloyd-George, who had been advised by his Chief of Staff that 'it would be madness to try and flatten the rebels', was convinced that whatever happened Ulster could not be coerced and certainly not by a British army.

Though originally Lloyd-George had intended the 1920 Act to apply throughout Ireland, the legislation became, in practice, the basis only for the Northern Ireland State. Northerners, when they examined their founding charter, saw little to enthuse them. Most unionists looked on what was on offer as, at most, an unhappy compromise diluting their position within the United Kingdom. For nationalists the proposals made them despair of their position. Separated from their co-religionists in the South, they felt isolated and vulnerable, symbolized by the creation of a land border and a Parliament in Belfast which they regarded, and were often encouraged by their unionist opponents to regard, as 'a Protestant Parliament for a Protestant People'.

Neither side had much confidence in the potential of the 'Partition Act' to survive. Nationalists in particular were to be cruelly encouraged into abstention tactics based on the erroneous notion that fundamental boundary changes and a Council of Ireland would make a nonsense of the new state of Northern Ireland. Northern nationalists simply could not accept the concept of partition as a permanent settlement. It was for them a traumatic shock which drove them into tactics which separated them from their Protestant fellow citizens at a moment of crucial debate in the form-ative years of the new state. So at a much later stage when constitutional nationalism abandoned its abstentionism, they entered a Parliament which had already legislated on vital community matters without the benefit of cross-community comment. As one eminent Southern academic has remarked:

> The initial phase of abstention was arguably a mistake because this was the foundation period of education and local government struc-tures. These important developments remained uninfluenced by minority participation and constructive criticism. Abstentionism also reinforced the apartheid mentality between Protestants and Cath-olics in every department of life.[5]

In the event, and in the absence of anything better on offer, Unionists accepted the Government of Ireland Act. As amended from time to time, the Act provided for Northern Ireland a first Constitution. To this day, and though overtaken by other Acts and Declarations, the 1920 Act has for many citizens a symbolism out of all proportion to any purpose it serves – it is seen as a seminal document. Mistaken though this emphasis may be, politicians need to tread warily in any rewriting exercises. But the fact remains that the Government of Ireland Act has been superseded in line with the changing needs of Northern Ireland, and never more so than in the extension of the consent principle giving the Northern people a deciding say in their constitutional future. So the much derided 'Parti-tion Act' of 1920, by the establishment of partition and developed by the consent principle, has made available a creative framework for long-term reconciliation in Ireland. Not many saw it that way and certainly the promise was well hidden in the politically sombre days of 1920.

One other great potential in the Government of Ireland Act was the way in which its authors, no doubt unwittingly, set in train the dismant-ling of inhibiting colonial structures which had been sacrosanct in the 120 years of the Act of Union. Partition, though it dismembered the island, released new forces and opened the way for the development of North/South home-grown institutions on which eventually new generations of Irish people would build. So halting steps were taken in the direction of island-based initiatives, albeit in separate jurisdictions, slackening the grip of London. Ironically, one of the 1969 criticisms directed at London by the Dublin Government was that Her Majesty's Government did not inter-fere *enough* in North Irish affairs – more, not less colonialism! Neither side got all they wanted in the 1920s legislation, but sufficient was on offer to persuade those who wished to govern to seek a mandate to do so.

A powerful factor in this persuasion process was the intervention of Edward Carson in the Commons debate in support of the partition scheme. Always reluctant to see Ireland divided and separated from the Imperial connection, Carson by 1920 had come to regard the setting up of an Ulster Parliament as the best defence of British citizenship. He made this clear in a key intervention in the Westminster debate in November 1920:

> The Ulster people having accepted the view of the Government that it was essential that they should be put under a Parliament of their own, which they did not ask for, have set themselves to get ready for that Parliament, and they have resolved and determined to work it in the best interests of their own country and of the Empire. I desire to say frankly to the House that I do see a great change in that direction in Ulster, and they are beginning to realise, now that they themselves will have charge of their own affairs . . . that if that Parliament is worked successfully and with goodwill, it may turn out more beneficial in their ordinary daily lives and in the local affairs of the country and may, under the scheme of the Bill, be able at the same time to protect in the closest degree the connection with this Parliament and with the United Kingdom as a whole. Therefore, so far as we are concerned, I am now even better fitted than before to give you the pledge that Ulster will do its best to perform the obligations put upon it under this Bill.[6]

Sir James Craig and other Unionists took their lead from Carson and moved quickly to fill the Ulster vacuum, taking also the advantage to confront the divided and dithering forces of Irish Nationalism with a *fait accompli*. Eventually any real threat of Southern intervention vanished, as a debilitating civil war in the Free State rendered the twenty-six counties incapable of any effective cross-border crusades.

Much was also done by the British administration to promote the implementation of the 1920 Act in at least one part of Ireland. A dramatic intervention by George V greatly helped the acceptance process when, in June 1921, the King spoke at the opening of the Northern Ireland Parliament in Belfast. It was a sombre occasion and the King, largely inspired by General Smuts of South Africa, used it as an opportunity to reach out in an ecumenical spirit of reconciliation. Throughout, the speech was inclusive in tone and content and was also superbly timed. 'By far the greatest service performed by a British monarch in modern times' was A. J. P. Taylor's judgement.

> 'I speak from a full heart', said the King, 'when I pray that my coming to Ireland today may prove to be the first step towards the end of strife among her people, whatever their race or creed. In that

hope I appeal to all Irishmen to pause, to stretch out the hand of forbearance and conciliation, to forgive and forget, and to join in making for the land they love a new era of peace, contentment and good will. It is my earnest desire that in Southern Ireland, too, there may, ere long, take place a parallel to what is now passing in this hall; that there a similar occasion may be performed. For this the Parliament of the United Kingdom has in the fullest measure provided. For this the Parliament of Ulster is pointing the way.'[7]

In reality the Ulster Parliament, Stormont, was anything but ready or willing to point the way. On the Unionist side, though there were considerable doubts about the viability of the system, Ulster showed itself, if not enthusiastic, at least ready, lest worse befall her, to work the Act.' Frank Pakenham, the author of *Peace by Ordeal* concluded that 'now at last it would be possible for a British Government to refuse to recognise any claim of Sinn Fein to speak for Ulster. Now at last Ulster was secure.'[8] Pakenham also noted that:

> though the British Cabinet (and the average Englishman) was convinced that North and South should be one the unity path was now barred alike by sentiment and solemn pledges. Ulster was now in a position to claim that the Partition Act was only accepted as a last and greatest sacrifice and on the explicit understanding that, unwelcome as it was to her, it at least made her safe for ever.[9]

Those realities became more recognizable as the smoke of civil war cleared. Ulster's part in yet another Great War underlined the special relationship with Britain and created circumstances in which no responsible body of British public opinion, and certainly no British Government, would attempt to force Northern Ireland out of the United Kingdom. Nowadays, even the British Labour Party with its 'United Ireland by consent' policy and its flirtation with a 'persuader' role for Government finds itself increasingly out of step with Irish public opinion, especially in the light of the Downing Street Declaration of December 1993. It is to be hoped that the Scottish ear of Tony Blair will listen more readily to the Irish who actually live in Ireland, as they seek to determine their future in ways that English advisers may not understand.

Equally, those who have used violence in pursuit of political aims in Northern Ireland since 1969 have made no progress in their attempt to reverse the partition imposed by the 1920 Act. The IRA allies of Sinn Fein may not have been beaten on the streets of Northern Ireland (nor were the security forces) when they declared a ceasefire in September 1994, but Mr Adams and his friends lost the battle that really counts – for the hearts and minds of the Irish people. After twenty-five years of violence, those who supported the Union had been given constitutional guarantees based on the most impressive coalition of support ever assembled in Anglo-Irish history.

Fortunately for Ireland, in 1920 there were pragmatic leaders in both new states who saw the necessity to accept responsibilities of government. Among such as these there was a rapid acceptance of the new facts of political life – above all, the existence of two states in Ireland. Each governance had a job to do and got on with it: partition became a fundamental factor which had to be accepted if the social fabric was to be maintained and improved.

For a while the Dublin leaders harboured the hope that a Boundary Commission would make changes to the detriment of the Northern State. Even that hope was dashed leaving a large Northern Catholic minority to fend for itself and to endure discrimination and hardship promoted by sectarian strife. So much so, in fact, that even when the post-1969 Northern crisis developed into a community confrontation which shocked the world, there was no great demonstration of effective intervention from the Republic. Nor was there likely to be.

One modern historian in the Republic had this to say about Southern concern for the North at the height of the 'troubles':

> To the contemporary observer in 1974, the Northern troubles had amazingly little impact on the South. There were, of course, such dramatic events as the resignation and dismissal of some of Mr Lynch's Ministers in May 1970 followed by a sensational arms trial. There were gunrunnings and rumours of gunrunning. There was the introduction of special criminal courts for the trial of IRA suspects, there were occasional tragic bombing incidents and there was some argument about Northern policy. But, by and large, there was no *popular* involvement, if we except the emotional outburst and the burning of the British Embassy in Dublin after Bloody Sunday in Derry. And there was no real indication (apart from the token gesture of deleting the 'special position' of the Catholic Church in Article 44) that the South wanted to change its constitution or its society to prepare itself for a new Ireland.

And then Professor Murphy asks this penetrating question:

> Had a homogeneous twenty-six county sovereign state developed to the point where it no longer wished to consider the radically disturbing implications of union of Catholic, Protestant and Dissenter?[10]

Twenty years on from that conclusion and conjecture the South has become even more aware and protective of its sovereignty. Constitutional forays that would endanger that sovereignty are frowned upon. Cross-border cooperation and guarantees for civil rights in the North are acceptable goals, but there is no evidence that the South wishes other than to act as a 'friend in court' for those in the North who look to them for sympathy. There is also no evidence that any electable Southern party (Sinn Fein collects a derisory vote in the South) is an advocate of republican aims which hark back to a distant era in Anglo-Irish politics and which for most Irish people can happily be left behind.

Even in August 1969 when the Catholics of Derry were desperately seeking outside help, all that strongly republican Taoiseach, Jack Lynch, could do in response was to make a national broadcast:

> Recognising . . . that (since) the reunification of the national territory can provide the only permanent solution for the problem, it is our intention to request the British Government to enter into early negotiations with the Irish Government to review the present constitutional position of the six counties of Northern Ireland.

In another, face-saving, gesture Mr Lynch also directed the Irish Army to have field hospitals established in Co. Donegal adjacent to Londonderry and at other points along the border to treat the injured who 'do not wish to be treated in six county hospitals'.[11] 'Is that the best he can do?' said Northern nationalists, who expected something more from one who, by giving fuel to the fire at such a critical moment, was adding to their difficulties. For militant loyalists it was grist to their mill. They squared-up to 'the enemy across the border' and made provision for loyalist reinforcements from Scotland, who were massing to join the battle should the Southern army do more than render first-aid.

A moment of truth had come: by 1969 (and long before it) the *de facto* policy of the South to the North had become effectively one of non-intervention. In 1969 in a momentary emotional spasm, Mr Lynch forgot the realities of the situation; very soon he and his successors were to move the argument to safer ground. Each new generation has confirmed that policy with renewed emphasis.

In the North, where society is far from homogeneous, the logic of partition is towards the creation of a pluralist society. Though often obscured by the traumatic effect of twenty-five years of paramilitary violence, something in the nature of a rainbow coalition is emerging in Northern Ireland as, slowly but surely, the main political establishments realize the need for communal unity. A new mix is being called for – Protestants who realize that partition can only work effectively if it has cross-community support and Catholics whose basic aim is peace with justice within Northern Ireland and a sharing of power in the structures of Government. Mr Major and Mr Reynolds, by agreeing the Downing Street Declaration, have responded to a people-promoted mood in Irish politics which has come to stay and demands attention.

The writers of the Government of Ireland Act 1920 could have fore-
seen none of this. At the time of its inception the Act was in most respects
a desperate response to a desperate situation. 'Getting round the next
corner' was the political order of the day. But out of the constitutional
chaos which followed the end of the Union in 1920 had come an Act
which, after much amendment and communal suffering, opened up the
prospect of a new order in Ireland – two states but one people.

The Irish were a bewildered people in the 1920s. Had they but known
it, they were being confronted by an idea whose time was coming. Succeeding chapters will point to 'markers' on the way in that transition.

REFERENCES AND NOTES

1 See David Bleakley, *Ireland and Britain, 1690–1990 – a Search for Peace*, Alex Wood
   Memorial Lecture, Fellowship of Reconciliation, 1982. See *Peace in Ulster*, ch.8, Mowbray, London, 1972, for a fuller discussion of this theme.
2 A.T.Q. Stewart, *The Narrow Ground* (Faber and Faber, 1977, especially Part Five).
3 *Ibid.*, p.164.
4 *Ibid.*, p.164.
5 John A. Murphy, *Ireland in the Twentieth Century* (Gill and Macmillan, 1975, p.156).
6 Carson, *H.C. Debates*, Cols 894–991, 1920.
7 Murphy, op.cit., p.25.
8 Frank Pakenham, *Peace by Ordeal* (Cape, 1985, p.78).
9 Pakenham, op.cit., p.105.
10 Murphy, op.cit., p.171.
11 Bew, P. and Gillespie, G., *North Ireland: a Chronology of the Troubles, 1968–1993* (Gill &
   Macmillan, 1993, p.18).

CHAPTER **5**

Ireland Act 1949 – Partition Confirmed

POLITICIANS IN IRELAND often behave like demented farmers: they pull up their country's constitutional roots from time to time, regardless of the consequences. Sometimes the results are disastrous; such was the case in 1948.

In that year John A. Costello managed to form a coalition government in Dublin with the prime aim of ending the long reign of de Valera. His tactic was to steal the master's clothes and to appear on the international stage as the true wearer of 'the green': he would leave the Commonwealth, declare Ireland a Republic and launch a worldwide onslaught on partition. It proved to be an extraordinary display of political opportunism and ineptitude. Many Irish people regarded the new policy as a disaster and said so. None more clearly than Tim Pat Coogan, one of Ireland's most astute political commentators: 'For most of 1949, instead of getting to grips with post-war social and economic problems the country was engulfed in the politics of retrospection.'[1]

Protestant reaction in the North to Mr Costello's proposals underlined the counter-productive nature of the initiative. Tensions rose, especially when it was announced that money raised at church door collections was to be used to promote anti-partitionist work and to support the campaigns of republican candidates in the forthcoming general election in Northern Ireland. The potential for sectarian strife was obvious: those who had struggled with some success to build bridges of reconciliation found their hopes 'butchered to make a Roman holiday' for the South.

This return to sectarian politics was a serious reversal, undoing the peacemaking work of a whole generation of Northerners who had advocated a politically ecumenical approach. The war years had promised much. There had been a peace 'spin-off' following the deepened personal contact between Protestants and Catholics in war service; equally, Labour victories in Britain encouraged a revival of radical non-sectarian politics in every area of Northern Ireland. Indeed, as the war came to an end impressive Labour and trade union rallies were held Provincewide. Packed political meetings (even on a Sunday) became a feature of Belfast's vast 'Hippodrome', with prominent speakers from the British 'left' holding centre stage. Herbert Morrison, Ernest Bevin, Hugh Dalton and Stafford Cripps were in popular demand. More surprisingly, the local Communist Party was also able to play to packed houses, with Willie Gallagher, MP, philosopher Palme Dutt or the 'Red Dean' of Canterbury topping the bill. Flag-waving, too, became less tribal, with the 'Hammer and Sickle' sharing pride of place alongside the Union Jack on many V-day Ulster buildings. The Unionist-controlled City Hall, not to be outdone, provided facilities for the famous 'Sword of Stalingrad' to be prominently displayed, to the delight of the thousands of citizens who filed past in respect. Joseph Stalin had many admirers in post-war Belfast!

In Ulster terms a revolution of rising social and political expectations had arrived, causing alarm bells to ring in Orange and Hibernian circles. Mr Costello's ill-judged initiatives destroyed all that. Not for the first time it was confirmed that 'when the South has a political sneeze, Ulster gets the cold'. Soon the 'backwoodsmen' of the 'right' in sectarian politics emerged from the shadowlands of politics which they had begun to occupy in post-1945 Ulster. Mr Costello had provided them with an agenda they understood – traditional *and* tribal. Such a divide was much more critical in its community effect than any that emerged in the South. The struggle in Dublin was about *who* should rule the state; in the North, in 1949, it was to be represented as a struggle for the very *existence* of the state. The 'demented farmers' were to have their way again in a frenzy of historical roots examination.

Already in the first post-war election the sectarian establishment had been given a considerable scare. The Labour Party in Belfast had won four seats in the Stormont Parliament and even in a staid middle-class area in Belfast the leader of Ireland's Communist Party had polled a formidable 5802 votes against one of the best known Unionist candidates. The countryside was moving, too, as rural seats were gained by radical non-sectarian candidates. A chance to stem the tide would attract traditionalists – Taoiseach John Costello provided that chance. But a policy of divide and conquer was always likely to weaken the already fragile sense of community in a less than thirty-year-old Province. All too easily would ancient fears be recalled. This proved to be the case when Sir Basil Brooke (later Lord Brookeborough) called a general election in February 1949 with the rallying cry: 'The border is the issue – say where you stand'.

The Prime Minister made his own special appeal, histrionic even by Irish standards:

> I ask you to cross the Boyne, if you like, with me as your leader and to fight for the same cause as King William fought in the days gone by. My friends, my soldiers, march with me. Your battle cry is 'No surrender, we are King's men'.[2]

Nationalists responded with equal inflammatory gusto – for a while there was a re-run of the electoral events of 1921.

I remember the occasion well. I was in my first year as a postgraduate student at Belfast's Queen's University at the time, when I surprised the Faculty by asking for time off to stand as a Northern Ireland Labour Party candidate in the Unionist stronghold of Victoria in East Belfast. It was my shipyard home area and my friends were anxious that I should contest in order to rally a cross-community vote at a time of sectarian polarization. Several of my colleagues from Oxford came over to help in the campaign – which was an occasion rather more turbulent than any likely to be encountered in electioneering in more sedate Southern England. More than words were exchanged in Election '49, as David Purdy, my valiant Election Agent often experienced to his discomfort.

It was my first time as a candidate and I was the youngest in the field. Two extracts from my Election Address give something of the cross-community appeal of the Labour and Trade Union Movement at a tense moment in political confrontation. They are also a reminder that as far back as 1949 there were people in Northern Ireland who recognized the consent principle and the need for community cooperation. Much which is accepted today as central to peacemaking was clearly visible in 1949 to those who wished to see. It was not necessary to go through the post-1969 trauma to reach such conclusions; we deplored the sectarian approach of establishment candidates.

These extracts indicate the cross-community approach offered by 'middle mandate' candidates in 1949. Much of what I had to say reflected my upbringing and the confirming experiences of shipyard and Oxford.

To the Electors of Belfast Victoria

February 1949.

Dear Friends,

February is a most unsuitable month on which to hold a General Election, and it may be that we will not have much opportunity to meet and talk over the issues which are foremost at this time. That being so I would like you to study this Address carefully for it may be your only opportunity to consider the Labour viewpoint.

To begin with, many of you may be wondering why it is that I, who have so many Unionist friends and relations, should be contesting Victoria on behalf of Labour. I first joined the Labour Party because I could no longer approve of what the Unionist Party was doing. We are taught in Ulster that the Christian way of life is the best life to lead, yet when I read and listened to the speeches of prominent Unionists I found that they preached hatred and strife.

Inside the Labour Party there was a new spirit. I found a policy and a tradition based on tolerance and goodwill. Instead of the bitter sectarianism which is the basis of Unionism I found that the Labour movement respected all, whatever their creed or calling.

It is with this attitude that we approach this election. The Unionists and Nationalists are doing their best to stampede the working people. We appeal to you to close the ranks. Do not let them divide us. They are afraid of the new demands which the workers are making, and this time we must show them that we approve of the social services introduced by the British Labour Government.

The Constitutional Position

Once again Sir Basil has had the audacity to declare that the border is to be the main issue in this election. We have heard this song before, and it is getting a bit monotonous. In case there may be some people who are unaware of the Labour Party's attitude to partition let me state it once again. First and foremost, it must be understood that the Labour Party is opposed to the Unionist Party AND the Nationalist Party. Our attitude has always been that we accept the constitutional position, and we have stated time and again that the border should remain so long as the majority of the people want it so. This is the policy of the British Labour Government, and it is the declared policy of the Northern Ireland Labour Party.

Of course the Unionists ignore these facts, and believing that any tune is better than no tune at all, they preach a policy which directs an undignified tirade against our fellow citizens. The Labour movement has never been party to such conduct. We contend that there is misery and hatred enough in the world without manufacturing more, and we deplore the fact that men who should know better insist on going out of their way to aggravate the unfortunate divisions which too often exist amongst us. In this election for Victoria the real issue is one of work for those without jobs, and houses for those without homes.

Unemployment

After housing we inevitably come to unemployment. Only those who have had this curse invade their own household can realise the suffering it brings in its train. Today more than 37,000 of our people are idle, and thousands more have been forced to seek work in England. If the Unionists talked less about the border and did something to solve this problem they would be doing the jobs they are paid to do. A Labour policy can solve unemployment; the Unionists have been trying for years but the only people who are assured of constant work are the clerks in the Labour Exchange.

Labour's Aim

The policy of the Northern Ireland Labour Party is the policy which is pursued by the Labour movements of all countries. We aim by organising the means of production to raise the standard of living to a point where men and women will be able to enjoy life in all its fullness. At the present time our Province is filled with insecurity and too many are being deprived of the opportunity to pursue the careers for which their talents and ambitions fit them. If you subscribe to these ideals, if you support the programme pursued by the British Labour Government, say so by voting Labour.

My Own Outlook

Personally, my own outlook is that of the Christian Socialism preached by Keir Hardie, Labour's greatest pioneer. It is a creed which attacks systems and not people. It is a way of life based on The Brotherhood of Man, and if adopted throughout our Province it would do much to heal the bitterness and intolerance which has crept into every aspect of our public life.

This is the Labour viewpoint. We are proud to proclaim it, and we invite all men and women to join with us in our Crusade to establish freedom from want, and freedom from fear.

Yours sincerely,
David Bleakley, February 1949

For those trying to establish non-sectarian politics in Northern Ireland the 1949 election was a disaster. The result reflected the reopened community divide. The trade union and labour gains of four years previously were wiped out with Unionists and anti-partition candidates consolidating their position. But it was no 'famous victory' for the people of Ulster of either tradition. Ulster voters had been pressed to take part in what was virtually a referendum on British citizenship – which at that relatively early stage in the formation of Northern Ireland meant a counting of

Protestant and Roman Catholic heads. Bridge-building candidates went largely unheard. However, and significantly, the result of the poll caused no lasting elation among the electorate. It had been, as they are called in Northern Ireland, a 'border election', in which social and economic matters of substance were given no hearing. Such pressing matters had been ignored in a politics of retrospection.

As I said at the end of my count in the City Hall: 'Today the Unionists are ringing their bells; one day they will be wringing their hands'.[3] However, I was one of the more fortunate Labour candidates – I actually saved my deposit! The intervention of Mr Costello, and particularly his stormy petrel, Sean MacBride, Minister for External Affairs, made a Unionist victory inevitable and provided the ruling party in Northern Ireland with a new catalogue of richly embarrassing quotations on which to base their conspiracy theory. Typical of these was MacBride's seal of approval on the 'Chapel Door' collection for republican funds. Many Roman Catholics were shocked by his effrontery and his maladroit handling of politically sensitive issues. But MacBride's clumsy appeal also revealed a serious out-of-touchness with Northern Protestants and Mac-Bride's longing to relive past battles:

> It is the first real sign of unity since 1921. I know that from glen to glen, parish to parish, from town to town the people of Ireland will look upon this development with hope and a throb in their hearts and will pray for its success.[4]

In reality, as an exercise in political obtuseness the Southern intervention in the 1949 Ulster election could not have been equalled. Certainly there *was* a response from every glen and parish in the North, but, at the end of the day, it was a Unionist response giving the Party its biggest-ever victory since the formation of the state. Worse still, it gave a boost to those whose trade in politics was sectarian, thereby delaying the day when a politics of partnership might emerge in which no false distinction would be drawn between person and person on the basis of religion. The constitutional crisis in the South also triggered off a series of consultations between Stormont and Westminster which in 1949 gave rise to new British legislation which in effect (and in contrast to Mr Costello's hopes and Sean MacBride's expectations) gave a permanency to partition far beyond the intentions of those responsible for the establishment of Northern Ireland in 1921. Costello's determination also involved the South in a withdrawal from the Commonwealth and so weakened further the sharing which they might develop with the North within that family of nations. Even de Valera saw the folly of such a break and showed his displeasure by absenting himself from the ceremony held to celebrate the departure. Such Southern behaviour emphasized the North–South divide; but the British Parliament's Ireland Act of 1949 confirmed the distinction and encouraged the gradual acceptance of an Ireland of *two* states. A theory of 'divided we stand' began to challenge the notion of 'Ireland divided never shall be free'.

However, in 1948 the immediate problem facing Clement Attlee's Labour Government was one of regularizing the tangled constitutional position facing the United Kingdom and the Commonwealth following the precipitative action of the Dublin Government. Fortunately for the South, the Republic was accorded what amounted to 'special relative' status. Attlee, ever a pragmatist, decided that the British and Irish peoples were so intertwined that it would be impossible to regard Irish citizens as foreigners – high ranking Members of Parliament and others in the British establishment would be affected. The Parliament Act of 1949 dealt with the problem in an eminently practical, if constitutionally unusual, way: Irish citizens, far from being given the foreign status Mr Costello's actions had seemed to invite, were in fact accorded privileges which allowed them to enjoy citizenship status, when living in Britain. To all intents and purposes, the right for citizens of the Republic to live and work in Britain and to enjoy the services of the social fabric of the community was established.

Sighs of relief were heard throughout the Republic when the Act was passed; they had feared Imperial retaliation. In was all a far cry from the trade wars of former days; it was also a tribute to the great common sense of Clement Attlee, a remarkable Labour Prime Minister, and his two Cabinet colleagues, Herbert Morrison and Chuter Ede. Morrison, in particular, was on close terms with his colleagues in the Northern Ireland Labour Party. He consulted us regularly and was anxious to ensure that nothing was done to weaken Northern Ireland's position inside the United Kingdom. He was also in touch with Unionist members at Stormont, and particularly with Edmund Warnock, a powerful member of the Parliamentary Party. Warnock, for his part, was most anxious to see that Northern Ireland's position inside the United Kingdom was not threatened or seen to be threatened by the withdrawal of Eire from the Commonwealth and its declaration of Republican status.

In the event, the Unionist Party had considerable cause for satisfaction. An important section of the Ireland Act 1949 specified:

> It is hereby declared that Northern Ireland remains part of His Majesty's dominions and of the United Kingdom and it is hereby affirmed that in no event will Northern Ireland or any part thereof cease to be part of His Majesty's dominions and of the United Kingdom without the consent of the Parliament of Northern Ireland.

So entered into Anglo-Irish and inter-Irish relations the concept of consent. The republicans in Dublin, by concentrating on republican 'purity', had fatally weakened their bargaining position and unwittingly helped to open a constitutional door of great potential in Ireland. Perhaps, deep down, there was an unconscious realization that two jurisdictions in Ireland might be no bad thing. Open discussion of such models of coexistence in 1949 was not fashionable (though otherwise in radical circles) among the political establishments. Such discussion would await the appearance of a new generation in the 1960s and 1970s, less trammelled by dogma.

Of supreme importance, the Act of 1949 by introducing the consent-for-change principle opened up a new approach to the 'border problem' in ways unthinkable thirty years previously. Doubly significant, and for Dublin hard to take, was the knowledge that this legislation came from a Labour Government traditionally influenced by a powerful Irish constituency in Britain. Later amending legislation has underlined the consent principle – the 1993 Downing Street Declaration and the 1995 Framework for the Future document are only the latest indications that the principle is now enshrined in constitutional law and supported by the most impressive coalition of support ever assembled in Anglo-Irish history. In effect the 1949 Ireland Act led to a questioning of much of the long-established 'conventional wisdom' on Irish unity matters. In the process many 'sacred cows' of Irish political life have been challenged, and all to the good.

In 1949 not many public persons in the Republic admitted to such changes or seemed aware of the possible long-term effect of their anti-partition propaganda. In reality the terms of the national argument had been changed dramatically. The presumed tentative nature of the constitutional divide in 1920 had given way to partition based on consent. And no bad thing – provided 'the people of Northern Ireland' meant something more than the narrow sectarian definitions offered, all too often, by those in authority.

From 1949 the Northern Ireland state has been, in respect to its ultimate constitutional integrity, every bit as sovereign as its Southern neighbour.

Lord Samuel recognized the sea-change that had taken place in North–South relationships as a result of the Labour Government's legislation, and Costello's ill-advised initiative. Speaking in the Lord's debate, this great Liberal statesman and long-standing friend of Ireland said:

> It would seem that the purpose of Eire in deciding to become an independent Republic was to secure the reunion of Ireland, but if they regarded that as a matter of importance, they had now taken the one step most calculated to defeat that purpose.[5]

Samuel's view was widely shared at the time; he recognized that a new and deeply significant die had been cast, to reshape the mould which had been broken by Eire's decision to become a Republic. But the newly added die of consent implied also a need for a radical change in attitude on the part of those who controlled the Northern Ireland state. Post-1920 politics had been propelled by the notion that there must be a Protestant Parliament for a Protestant people – defended in large part by the argument that the 1921 settlement had been the outcome of a head count of Protestants and Catholics. 'Consent' demanded a higher order of thinking. So, though not clearly acknowledged or recognized in 1949, what was now being required of Northern Irish politicians was the development of a new polity, inter-communal and non-sectarian in thrust.

The year 1920 had provided a focus for division in Northern Ireland. Thirty years later, in a changed national and international environment, there was the opportunity for those of a new generation to reach out to one another, seeking together the creation of a United Ulster – Catholic, Protestant and Dissenter, one for all and all for one. That was the awesome challenge which faced the Northern Ireland people as they entered the second half of the twentieth century after the 1948 Ireland Act.

In Samuel Beckett's phrase, Northern Ireland was now between 'a death and a difficult birth'. The real journey into peace had begun; plans for the future were being exchanged across old divides. 'Future tense' people, and particularly Young Ulster, began to sense that Northern Ireland had the capacity to become a place at peace with itself and at ease with its neighbours. The growing acceptance of the consent principle would make all this possible.

REFERENCES AND NOTES

1   Timothy Patrick Coogan, *Ireland Since the Rising* (Pall Mall Press, 1966, p.96 and especially Chapter 5).
2   David Bleakley, *Faulkner* (Mowbray, 1974, p.41).
3   David Bleakley, Diary, February, 1949.
4   David Bleakley, *Faulkner* (Mowbray, 1974, p.42).
5   Timothy Patrick Coogan, op.cit., p.97.

PART THREE

FOUNDING FATHERS

CHAPTER 6

The Legacy of Carson

B Y COMMON CONSENT Sir Edward (later Lord) Carson was Ulster's chief advocate in its initial battle for separate survival – in Terence O'Neill's phrase, 'the dramatic spokesman of the Unionist cause'.

Born in Dublin on 9 February 1854, Edward Carson, after a Trinity College education, became a QC at thirty-five. In a few years he was acknowledged as one of the greatest advocates of his day, and particularly at the English Bar. His contemporaries noted the amalgam of gifts which combined to make him special: 'His virulent invective, his uncanny skill in laying traps for unwary feet, his power of making witnesses say ridiculous things by an almost diabolical mastery of the arts of cross-examination, his superb power of seeing the one essential point in a case, his courage in abandoning everything else and in staking the whole issue perhaps on a single question'[1] – all these qualities pointed up Carson's outstanding ability.

Yet, at first glance, Edward Carson seemed an odd choice to lead Ulster's cause. At fifty-seven, and in failing health, he had spent the best years of his life in the legal world and knew little about the Northern Province. But, once asked, Carson found the challenge to take up the Ulster brief irresistible. Rather like Enoch Powell in a later generation, he saw a profound Imperial significance in what was at stake and felt 'strangely drawn' to address the issue.

Nor did Carson lack confidence in his ability to take on such a seemingly impossible brief; indeed he was known to be attracted by such challenges. Supremely certain, and not a little arrogant, he was proud of the Protestant stock from which he had come and deeply aware of the contribution which his people had made to nation and empire. With W. B. Yeats, he was ever ready to demonstrate that the Protestants of

Ireland were not petty people, and would have approved of the poet's later protest to the Irish Senate:

> We are the people of Burke; we are the people of Grattan; we are the people of Swift, the people of Emmet, the people of Parnell. We have created most of the modern literature of this country. We have created the best of its political intelligence.[2]

That same political intelligence confronted Carson with an awesome conclusion: the maintenance of the Union between Ireland and Britain was essential if the integrity of the Empire was to be protected. By such standards the Liberal proposals for Home Rule in Ireland were anathema and had to be opposed by all means possible. He also felt it a point of honour to be available should the call come to lead the Ulster people. That call came in 1910; from then to the establishment of the Northern Ireland Parliament in 1921, Carson formulated the strategies of the Province; he was the chief public defender of its cause; and he was the symbol of its defiance.

Once committed to lead the Ulster Unionists Carson moved swiftly to establish his authority and to develop his plans. In a series of dramatic public meetings in the Province in 1911, a high proportion of the population was informed of what was at stake and what would be required of them. Carson, aided by his powerful analytical and oratorical skills, got quickly to the heart of the matter and spelled out with unmistakable clarity what he wanted his followers to do. Coming from a pillar of the English legal establishment the message was breathtaking in its implications:

> 'Our demand', he said 'is a very simple one. We ask for no privilege, but we are determined that no one shall have privilege over us. We ask for no special rights, but we claim the same rights from the same Government as every other part of the United Kingdom. We ask for nothing more; we will take nothing less. It is our inalienable right as citizens of the British Empire, and Heaven help the men who try to take it from us.'

This was the first of many 'Ulster will fight and Ulster will be right' pronouncements – they left little room for ambiguity. As he told his audiences incessantly and warned Parliament constantly, Ulster would not be coerced. This meant being prepared to be responsible for the government of what he began to describe as 'the Protestant Province of Ulster'.[3]

By the Government's standards such suggestions amounted to treason. Carson rebutted such accusations by reminding the Government that he viewed its actions as unconstitutional. He pointed, in particular, to the way in which separation from Britain would impair Ulster's United Kingdom citizenship, as well as her high position in the British Empire. So the parameters for a possible revolt were being delineated and a justification given. More dangerously, a rebellious thought had been implanted in minds less subtle than his which succeeding generations of Unionists would keep in reserve as a last resort for a 'doomsday' situation.

Carson also needed to prove to the world that he had provincewide support for his challenge to Westminster. He achieved this through a sensational event – a special 'Ulster Day' was announced for 28 September 1912. It turned out to be a day of massive and ominous constitutional significance. The people of Ulster were asked to assemble at Belfast's City Hall to sign a Covenant of their intent to resist any threat to their United Kingdom citizenship. The response was a biggest-ever (some half-million) rally at which 237,368 men and 234,046 women signed an historic declaration of defiance and commitment, some with their own blood. By any standard it was a momentous occasion, threatening, exciting and awesome. Those in Ulster who were not born at the time were brought up on many stories and interpretations (sometimes conflicting according to the family of origin!) about the Day.

The Covenant was a carefully worded appeal, reflecting Carson's calculated balance between protestations of loyalty to the Monarch and Empire and warnings about a government conspiracy against the Empire. To this day the famous document is an honoured family heirloom framed on many an Ulster Unionist living room wall:

ULSTER'S
Solemn League and Covenant

BEING CONVINCED in our consciences that Home Rule would be disastrous to the material well-being of Ulster, as well as of the whole of Ireland, subversive of our civil and religious freedom, destructive of our citizenship and perilous to the unity of the Empire, we, whose names are underwritten, men of Ulster, loyal subjects of His Gracious Majesty King George V, humbly relying on the God whom our fathers in days of stress and trial confidently trusted, do hereby pledge ourselves in solemn Covenant throughout this our time of threatened calamity to stand by one another in defending for ourselves and our children our cherished position of equal citizenship in the United Kingdom and in using all means which may be found necessary to defeat the present conspiracy to set up a Home Rule Parliament in Ireland. And in the event of such a Parliament being forced upon us we further solemnly and mutually pledge ourselves to refuse to recognise its authority.

In sure confidence that God will defend the right we hereto subscribe our names. And further, we individually declare that we have not already signed this Covenant.

28 September 1912.

The comprehensiveness of the Covenant, its solemnity of language, and the backing it received left no doubt in the mind of the government in London about the strength of public concern harnessed by Carson. From then on it was generally accepted that Belfast and London were on a collision course. In the year which followed, both sides made military preparations for a battle which neither wanted, while at the same time desperate political negotiations went on behind closed doors.

By the summer of 1914 a 'high noon' was approaching, with Carson giving vent to the feeling of melancholy which weighed on his spirits: 'I see no hopes of peace. I see nothing at present but darkness and shadows – we must be ready. In my own opinion the great climax and great crisis of our fate, and the fate of our country, cannot be delayed for many weeks – unless something happens – when we shall have once more to assert the manhood of our race.'[4]

But for those concerned in the Anglo-Irish debate in 1914 an even greater event – the declaration of war against Germany – intervened. Suddenly there was in Ireland a perceived need to unite against a more obvious common enemy. The transformation was extraordinary. Neither Carson nor his lifelong nationalist opponent, John Redmond, were willing to make an opportunity out of England's difficulty; they did not wish to purchase concessions by selling their wider patriotism.

North and South, the call went out – 'Your country and Empire need you'. Throughout Ireland those who had been preparing to wage war against one another were enjoined to 'fight the Hun'. They did so in vast numbers (some 132,000), and for a while set aside domestic difficulties with, perhaps, a sigh of relief.

Carson's sense of patriotism was afterwards acknowledged by Prime Minister Asquith, when he paid tribute to the valour of the Ulster Volunteer Force – the coercion of the Province became increasingly unthinkable as battles like those of the Somme forged fresh bonds of mutual respect and indebtedness. Redmond, marginalized by his republican opponents, died in 1918, worn out by his efforts on behalf of his people. He got little thanks from the British Government for his strenuous efforts on behalf of Ireland, Britain and Empire. In the end, in the words of one of his biographers 'Redmond was carried away "in the gale of the world" and his name no more held in high esteem among his Irish people.'[5]

By the end of the Great War (rather as after 1945) Ulster's position in the British family had been greatly strengthened. Lloyd-George increasingly appreciated this mood with its obvious implications that Ulster must be given a 'favoured Province' status in any new Ireland. A logic of partition was emerging, morally and politically. Eventually a proposal for such a guarantee was offered and legislation to safeguard the six north-east counties of Ulster was passed in 1920. In an ironic comment on the compromise, Carson suggested: 'It may well turn out that the only part of Ireland which will have a Parliament is the part which never asked for it.'[6]

There is also evidence from that same debate that Ulster's Unionists were getting used to the notion of partition and beginning to count up its advantages. An intervention by Charles Craig, MP and brother of Ulster's first Prime Minister, gives some idea of the new thinking, far removed in some essentials from Carson's approach:

> It has been said that this Bill lends itself to the union of Ulster and the rest of Ireland. It would not be fair to the rest of this House if I lent the slightest hope of that union arising within the lifetime of any man in this House. I do not believe it for a minute.

Nor would the speaker contemplate bringing in the three excluded counties of Ulster – Monaghan, Cavan and Donegal – to the proposed six-county state. Such a suggestion, once discussed by Carson, could eventually upset the political arithmetic. To Charles Craig the danger was clear – he feared a revenge of the cradle. He had done his sums:

> The three excluded counties contain some 70,000 Unionists and some 260,000 Sinn Feiners and Nationalists, and the addition of that large block of Sinn Feiners and Nationalists would reduce our majority to such a level that no sane man would undertake to carry on a Parliament with it. A couple of Members sick, or two or three Members absent for some accidental reason might in one evening hand over the entire Ulster Parliament and the entire Ulster position, for which we have fought so hard and so long, to Captain Redmond and his friends – and that, of course, is a dreadful thing to contemplate.[7]

Charles Craig had, indeed, done his sums, but they were deeply divisive calculations.

One wonders what the eventual course of Ireland might have been had Nationalists in earlier years warmed to Edward Carson's suggestion that nine, instead of six, counties might be the ideal boundary of an agreed exclusion zone. But by 1920 the counting of heads on a tribal basis was well on the way as Parliament prepared to give the six counties of the north-east the measure of protection through partition now sought by the Ulster Unionists.

Having reached agreement at Westminster, Carson was coming to the end of his centre-stage role in Ulster politics. In ten years of leadership he had argued successfully for the brief he had accepted in 1911; and he had secured for himself a Founding Father place in the history of the Province. Now he was ready to move on and leave the labours of state building to others with more appropriate skills. As he laid down his responsibilities, Carson was up-beat in his expectations and felt able to assure the Commons that Ulster would do its best to make the new Act work.

But Carson was also capable of assessing the difficulties that confronted the new state which he had done so much to create. He recognized that an historic turning point had been reached in North–South relations in Ireland and inside the six Northern Counties. Aware, no doubt, that unpredictable forces had been set loose in Ulster (and which he had helped to set loose) he gave those who were to rule the people he had led a warning which they would ignore at their peril:

> I say to those of you who for so many years have trusted me in the North of Ireland – whose Parliament is going, I believe, to be set up – I tell them that they will have the greatest opportunity of showing the reality of their professions of loyalty towards your Empire by displaying in their acts of government a tolerance, a fairness, and a justice towards all classes and toward all religions of the community. They must forget faction and section and they must resolve to govern the community over which they are placed in such a way as will show that they are the worthy citizens of this Empire that I believe them to be.[8]

It was sound advice, but a lot to expect from the bewildered followers whom he was shortly to leave. Carson had led Ulster's Unionists to the constitutional brink in their battle with the British Government; and he had stoked up fires of provincial loyalty and religious traditions. In so doing, he had alienated most of Ireland's Roman Catholics. Now without his personal presence Ulster Unionists were required to reach an accommodation with these same Roman Catholic fellow citizens who on many occasions had been branded by Carson as untrustworthy. Partition in 1921 was an established fact of constitutional life, but a fact not yet acknowledged by either nationalist or republican politicians, North and South. Unionists, too, were uncertain about the future and had yet to consolidate their gains.

But Carson's place as the founder of Northern Ireland as a political unit was assured. Yet, as one eminent contemporary observed, 'the foundation of Northern Ireland was not the object for which he fought: it represents a compromise after a long and grim struggle, but it was a compromise which never could have been made without the devotion, the courage, and the judgement of Edward Carson.'[9]

Nevertheless, it was a grim legacy which Carson handed on in 1921 to his carefully chosen successor, Sir James Craig, later Lord Craigavon. The 'dramatic spokesman of the Unionist cause' was being replaced by someone more taciturn, but no less stubborn and determined to succeed.

REFERENCES AND NOTES

1   See Edward Marjoribanks, *The Life of Lord Carson* (Victor Gollancz, 1932, especially Chapter 1).
2   Brian Inglis, *The Story of Ireland* (Faber and Faber, 1956, p.238).
3   John F. Harbinson, *The Ulster Unionist Party, 1882–1973* (Blackstaff Press, 1973, p.27).
4   *Belfast News Letter*, 24 July 1914.
5   Nicholas Mansergh, 'John Redmond', in *The Shaping of Modern Ireland* (Routledge and Kegan Paul, 1960, p.48).
6   Harbinson, op.cit., p.30.
7   *Ibid.*, p.30 and p.31 and especially Chapters 1–4 of this standard history for the period.
8   Carson, *H.C. Debates*, Col.1442–43, Vol.134.
9   Marjoribanks, op.cit., p.2.

CHAPTER 7

Premiers Three: Craig, Andrews, Brooke (1921–1963) 'Not an Inch' – Not Enough

CARSON'S PARTING WORDS OF WARNING and encouragement to Ulster's new rulers were well chosen – one wonders what would have happened had he felt able to continue in leadership in the formative days of the new state. Would his massive authority have been sufficient to hold in check the dangerously sectarian emotions engendered by the resistance campaign which he had so assiduously promoted a few years earlier?

And another 'if' of history: what would have happened if the earlier phases of nationalist abstentionist policy had been more selective in application. Most Catholics were reluctant to give any credence to the new state, as those who did so were often dubbed 'Castle Catholics'. A later generation of nationalist historians have made the point that 'the initial phase of abstention was arguably a mistake because this was the period which saw the foundation of education and local government structures. These important developments remained uninfluenced by minority participation and constructive criticism'. The same Professor of Irish history from Cork University also makes the point that leaders of *both* communities did little to improve the harsh sectarian atmosphere. For example: 'Lord Craigavon's notorious phrase "a Protestant Parliament for a Protestant People" was matched by Cardinal MacRory's egregious utterance that the Protestant Churches did not form part of the true Church of Christ'. He continues: 'Catholics and Protestants kept themselves rigorously segregated in education and it is difficult not to regard the division of children as being a major factor in perpetuating the enmities of adults'.[1]

Whatever the reasons, the 'apartness' in Ulster society was fatally underlined in the early days of state-building and scant regard was paid to the views of those who tried to create cross-community structures which might stem the sectarian tide. Even modest gains by middle man-date candidates were frowned upon by the Unionist Party, and the government sought to make more certain of its already considerable majority by abolishing proportional representation for parliamentary elections in 1929. For those promoting a policy of 'spurning flags and seeking bread' the 1920s and 1930s were hard years in which to get a hearing. Unionists who wished to preserve the status quo had little to worry about, provided they banged the appropriate sectarian drum. Labour leaders, nationally, regularly exposed this strategy and pleaded in vain for working-class unity. So, inevitably, Ulster (like its Southern neigh-bour) lost contact with non-Irish mainstream politics. Labour leader Ram-sey McDonald's analysis was apt when he told Westminster:

> In Belfast you get labour conditions the like of which you get in no other town, no other city of equal commercial prosperity from John O'Groats to Land's End or from the Atlantic to the North Sea. It is maintained by an exceedingly simple device . . . Whenever there is an attempt to root out sweating in Belfast the Orange big drum is beaten.[2]

In fact, in the early days of the Stormont administration the border issue was a political lifesaver for Orange and Green establishments alike at election times. Without this emotion-raising fixation Ulster's traditional politicians might have found difficulty in resisting the demands of mili-tant ex-servicemen who, Protestant and Catholic together, were aware of the lead being given in Britain by former battlefield comrades who had successfully assaulted the Tory political heartlands of Scottish and English industrial cities. Such a class confrontation would have been infinitely more healthy for the Province than the blatantly sectarian self-protection schemes designed to favour a social status quo.

In the event, most politicians in the formative years of Northern Ire-land took no chances where political bridge-building was concerned. They kept one another at arm's length, each to his or her own political ghetto. Cross-community groups were regarded as being 'neither one nor the other', 'not to be trusted', 'not quite part of the national order of things'. This view has not been eradicated from North Irish politics but it is increasingly challenged by a growing body of Ulster people who practise a pluralism that is both pragmatic and progressive. But in the early days of Northern Ireland the prevailing mood was one of self-preservation, with one side (Protestant) determined not to surrender 'an inch' of their Six

Counties; and the other side, nationalist in conviction and in traumatic shock (Catholics) fervently believing that something would 'turn up' to establish Ireland as 'a nation once again'. Additionally, each community was plagued by a 'double minority' calculation, which gave Protestants a majority in the partitioned state, but made Catholics a majority in an all-island context. Such sectarian arithmetic encouraged an unhealthy consciousness of kind.

Sir James Craig, 1921–1940

Such was the political ethos of the Six-County state (Fermanagh, Armagh, Tyrone, Londonderry, Antrim and Down) when Sir James Craig (later Lord Craigavon), at the age of fifty, became Ulster's first Prime Minister in 1921. Few envied him his task but, unlike Carson, he was well prepared to lead his party in the new Parliament (Stormont, as it was and is more commonly known). Craig's local roots went deep and he had already a considerable parliamentary career behind him at Westminster as Member for East Down since 1906. His immense wealth, combined with great energy and ability, had enabled him to devote his full time to politics and he was widely favoured for high office within the Conservative Party. But once Carson decided that it was time to return to his first love of law, Craig was the choice of Ulster's unionists; he responded readily to their unanimous call to serve.

By any standard the task was daunting, but, greatly encouraged by George V's speech at the opening of the new Parliament in June 1921, Craig applied himself to what he regarded as the priorities dictated by circumstances.

There was no blueprint to follow, but some idea of the new Premier's professed 'feel' for the task was revealed in his opening speech to Parliament. Much of what he said echoed the sentiments offered by Carson's farewell guidelines for those who would govern Northern Ireland. Craig, too, was comprehensive in his appeal, placing himself and his colleagues 'at the disposal of the Northern Ireland people'. All citizens were assured that there would be 'nothing meted out to those but the strictest justice'. None need be afraid, but he continued that 'the laws must be obeyed'. There was also a promise that his government would be absolutely 'honest and fair in administering the law'.[3] How, then, was the promise fulfilled?

Public opinion has been kinder to Craig than to many of his more flamboyant successors. And, of course, starting with a clean sheet, administration-wise, his practical achievements draw attention away from some of his more serious errors of judgement and defects in basic political philosophy. A more recent Premier, Terence O'Neill, had no doubts about the importance of Craig's contribution and its centrality to the creation of Northern Ireland. Speaking from the perspective of 1968, O'Neill concluded:

Craigavon's great achievement was to bring our institutions of government into being and give them a quality to endure. Let us remember that he set out with a government that had no staff to serve it, no officers, no traditions, no certainty of survival . . . Carson may well have been the dramatic spokesman of the Ulster cause, but Craigavon was the hard-working and determined builder of our government institutions.[4]

Ironically, O'Neill's 'quality to endure' comment was offered one year before 1969 when the institutions of the state he was commending would begin to fall apart – solid bricks had been laid, but the essential social cement was missing.

Terence O'Neill's stress on administrative competence is also significant in that it admires Craig as an outstanding technocrat, inspiring his colleagues and a dedicated team of able civil servants with the thrust of his priorities. Unfortunately, however, those priorities became the priorities of the whole Stormont regime and excluded issues which were even more central to the survival of the state. Ulster was centred on a 'political arithmetic' which left no room for the higher political calculus which leaders of deeply divided states must always address if they are to create a viable community.

In his own day Craig was widely regarded by his supporters as the solid rock (and he reigned for nineteen years) on which Ulster was founded and which he came to symbolize. His biographer, St John Ervine, describes him as 'a destined man . . . for a definite purpose and a definite period' – *Craigavon: Ulsterman* as he entitled the biography. But Craig's definition of Ulster was incomplete. He and his colleagues never seemed to understand the paramount need for inter-communal unity and for institutions to promote that unity. Certainly the Prime Minister observed protocol in official Roman Catholic/State relations and was often rebuffed for doing so; but his stress on his Protestantism and his boast of being an Orangeman first and a member of Parliament afterwards made pointless and hollow-sounding much of the exercise and widened the already disastrous division between Northern Protestants and Catholics. Most serious of all, Ulster's first Premier created a model of government which his immediate successors found difficult to reverse or were happy to perpetuate. No doubt Craig felt constrained by the conditions of his time, but in his position of near absolute political power he was uniquely placed to advance community healing initiatives. It was not enough to insist that what was being provided by government was, in law, available to all: if one-third of the population felt excluded by the state system there was a problem to address.

Craig's reign was long (1921–1940) and his achievements were considerable, but the central fact remains that neither he nor his colleagues addressed the real problem of Ulster politics – the need to give the new state a foundation of cross-community support. This was the core issue which Lord Craigavon left for his immediate successors to address. They were freer to do so in a world more open to change than that of an earlier generation – unfortunately their response to the challenge was inadequate.

John Miller Andrews, November 1940–May 1943 – a term too short

J. M. Andrews, very much Ulster's unknown Prime Minister, slipped into office almost unnoticed, following the sudden death of Lord Craigavon in November 1940. For the Province the death of its first Premier was a shattering blow, compounded by the growing uncertainties of war. In such circumstances reassurance was sought – honest 'J.M.' (born in the same year as Craigavon) was on hand to ensure continuity.

But Andrews had more formidable qualifications than being merely available. Born into a wealthy Co. Down industrial family in 1917, 'J.M.' was steeped in politics from an early age and, through the connections of his family with Lord Pirrie and the Liberal Unionists, shared links with one of Britain's most powerful industrial and political networks. Andrews was also a familiar figure among civil servants in Northern Ireland and Britain, and holding cabinet rank since 1921 he was well versed in the handling of legislative matters. Furthermore, his ministries of Labour and Finance were among the more practical in the affairs of the Province. For such reasons Andrews, though a loyal member of the Unionist Party, was regarded by many outside Unionism, and particularly in the trade union and business world, as the most approachable of Ministers. So much so, indeed, that early in the war he had hoped for a Northern Ireland parallel to the wartime truce established between Tories and Labour in Britain.

Andrews' greatest claim to fame (and it remains of paramount significance in London–Ulster relations) was to persuade the British Government to accept that Northern Ireland should enjoy the principle of parity of treatment in social services – a crucial principle in view of the great extension of the welfare state, post-war. Parity of treatment ('step-by-step' as it came to be called) was also supplemented by provision for special 'leeway' grants to enable catching-up in problem areas of social development.

Such practical developments pioneered by J. M. Andrews did much to cement the Union and in ways which joined Northern Ireland's citizens in common cause. Less abrasive than his predecessor and with a wider experience than most of his colleagues Andrews, if he had been given more time, might have presented a more acceptable face of Unionism. But in the heady days of wartime Ulster in 1943 such considerations counted little with a young guard of Unionists who wanted to portray the

image of a party vigorously engaged in the war effort and, equally important, anxious to maintain a Unionist–Conservative status quo in the likeli-
hood of a post-war Labour government. However, many close observers
of Ulster politics would agree with the judgement of the leading historian
of the Unionist Party that, had Andrews been allowed to continue his
social and economic planning for post-war Ulster, 'then the subsequent
history of Northern Ireland may have been much more peaceful and
prosperous'.[5] But time was not on the side of J. M. Andrews – his replace-
ment was waiting impatiently in the wings.

Sir Basil Brooke, 1943–1963

When Sir Basil Brooke (later Lord Brookeborough), after a good deal of
in-fighting, took over from Andrews, there was a general feeling that a
new generation had arrived in politics. Brooke, whose tenure of office was
to span some of the most significant war and post-war developments, had
a firm political power base on which to work. Equally attractive and
reassuring to his Party was his background: landed gentry from Co. Fermanagh, Winchester and Sandhurst, distinguished war service and, invaluable in wartime, a close family and personal connection with
Churchill's military advisers – Alanbrooke, Montgomery, Alexander, Dill,
Cunningham and many others with Irish connections. Equally formidable
was the support of his English-born wife, Lady Cynthia – ever active
behind the scenes and prone to lecture Cabinet Ministers – something of
a 1940s Ulster version of Hilary Clinton! All these were considerable
advantages. What, then, went wrong?

Basically, Sir Basil Brooke was content to coast along a traditional
course. In particular, he showed little interest in moving Northern Ireland in the direction of the new pluralism which wartime experience was
encouraging in United Kingdom society. Like most of his Party he was
unable to read the signs of his time and get rid of the historical baggage
which was hindering progress inside the Province. In addition, the war
itself and the excitement of post-war expansion in government services
produced a political flurry which helped to push into a 'future agenda'
more deep-seated communal issues which required instant attention.
'Rocking the boat' was not encouraged.

A man of great urbanity, Brooke was at the same time ever ready to
play to his Unionist gallery and to lambast any who introduced what he
regarded as a foreign culture into local unionist and conservative politics.
He could be blunt in expression, hence one of his memorable outbursts
against Prime Minister Attlee's socialist intentions: 'Only a bloody fool
would vote Labour!' For a short time in the 1940s when the number of
'bloody fools' in Ulster grew rapidly, there were even suggestions by some
disturbed Unionists that dominion status might be a way out of Attlee's
socialist commonwealth. But Brooke was also a realist and Ulster people,

Protestant and Catholic alike, knew that the issue of the 'half-crown' was every bit as important as that of the 'Crown'. So Ulster got its welfare state under its Tory–Unionist Premier.

It was a great advance. Arguably the most significant community-binding event in the history of Northern Ireland, the welfare state made nonsense of much of the social separation of the past; in the act of creating the new service and, above all, in benefiting from it, a community oneness was created which cut across the notion of a political/religious sectarian divide. The citizens of Northern Ireland no longer saw themselves as belonging to neat 'orange' or 'green' categories – new blends were emerging. All were equal on 'Giro day'.

Here then was a unique opportunity for Brooke to build upon. But once again he did not respond and when in doubt resorted to sectarian partisanship. Sometimes his initiatives in this direction were reckless and damaging to community relations. As we have noted earlier, in the 1949 general election following Eire's withdrawal from the Commonwealth there was a return to '1690' rhetoric. The eve-of-poll Election Manifesto published by the Unionist leader gives some idea of the 'heady' nature of his appeal at a tense moment in Ulster affairs. In tone it was calculated to raise the political temperature by arousing old fears and to produce a greatest-ever pro-Union Protestant response; it succeeded in both respects:

Election Manifesto 1949 – message from the Prime Minister –

Our country is in danger. We are fighting to defend our very existence and the heritage of our children.

The British Government will abide by the decision we make together. Therefore our loyalty must be overwhelmingly affirmed.

In the Dail the other day a gentleman said the gun would be used. We are not going to be scared.

We are perfectly capable of looking after ourselves.

I want to assure you that the Government will see to it that law and order will be maintained.

We are a friendly people, but we are not going to be threatened.

We are not going into a Gaelic state.

We are not going to ask our children to learn a Gaelic language.

We are not going to have lower social services.

We shall defend Ulster with the last bit of life left in us.

So I call on you to give an answer to our opposition at the poll that will resound throughout the world.

That answer will be 'No Surrender'.[6]

Even allowing for the tensions of 1949 this was colourful language, but there is no evidence that any of the bright young men recruited by

Unionist headquarters wished to modify the leader's appeal. Worse still, Sir Basil was sending the wrong signals to the reinvigorated post-war Unionist Party which he was creating. 'Follow the Leader' became the watchword for most; some more far-seeing Unionists simply kept their heads down and got on with their political agenda as best they could, while admitting in private that they wished it could be otherwise.

Like Craig, with whom he had great rapport, Sir Basil Brooke encouraged his Ministers to get on with the business of developing the economy and strengthening the infrastructure of the Province. However, when he was prepared to be 'his own man', Brooke displayed both talent and political 'clout'. He did so impressively when in 1949 he persuaded Prime Minister Attlee to include in the Ireland Act of that year guarantees that Northern Ireland would remain an integral part of the United Kingdom unless the Parliament of Northern Ireland decided otherwise. The principle of 'consent' was enshrined in the Constitution giving a copperbottom to the legislation of 1920.

But even here Brooke's victory was deemed tribalist and much of his own comments on the event was 'tribal' in tone; the community consensus dimension was, as always, missing. During the succeeding decade Lord Brookeborough, as he became, was more and more content to rest on his 1949 laurels and leave the generation of new ideas for unionism in the hands of the talented younger team with which he had surrounded himself. What he forgot was that these followers, often with an eye on future leadership, were not likely to endanger that future by treading on what was regarded as the 'thin ice' of community reconciliation. Indeed, even the few who suggested a modest step forward – the recruitment of Roman Catholics into membership of the Unionist Party – had to retreat in disarray, unprotected by their Prime Minister. The decisive leadership needed in such sensitive areas was not given and there were no rivals in the field.

Sir Basil Brooke's long Premiership owes much to the style of government which he brought to Stormont. This style was appreciated by most who served under him. A notable and surprising exception was Terence O'Neill, a trusted and favoured member of Brookeborough's inner circle. O'Neill in his 1972 autobiography, and while his old leader was still alive, delivered a hurtful judgement which gave great offence at the time and highlighted what many regarded as a typical example of insensitivity in human relationships with his colleagues:

> I think I should say a word about my predecessor, Lord Brookeborough. He was a man of immense personal charm. He was good company and a good raconteur and those who met him imagined that he was away from his desk. What they didn't realise was that there was no desk.

A man of limited intelligence, his strong suits were shooting and fishing in Fermanagh and when he came up on Monday night or Tuesday morning it was difficult to shake him from some of his more idiotic ideas. In short, it would have been quite impossible even with his immense charm, for him to have been a minister in London.[7]

Ulster's oldest surviving member of Brooke's administration and last Speaker of the Parliament of Northern Ireland, Sir Ivan Neill (born 1906), does not agree with Terence O'Neill's assessment of Brookeborough. Neill sees the 'laid back' style as part of the success story and never to be discounted. In fact he believes that Terence O'Neill might have been more successful if in *his* style of government he had taken more note of his predecessor's methods. Writing in his 'Memoirs' (unpublished, as yet) Neill has this to say:

> None should underestimate the contribution Sir Basil made to Ulster, particularly to her security within the United Kingdom. A gentleman loyal to his colleagues, he chose his Ministers, let them know what he expected from them then left them to get on with the job, but was at their side when trouble arose. Sir Basil was a country gentleman, fishing and shooting were part of his life and he had the facilities of his estate at Colebrooke to enjoy. He was able to combine his enjoyment of these with his duties as Prime Minister, and this was where he was misunderstood. He knew that he could rely on his Ministers to keep the wheels of Government turning, but public opinion generally expected to see more of his presence at Stormont. The fact is he was able to do both successfully. His method of government was quite unique: he governed by influence and did so successfully. A more skilled statesman than Sir Basil without the influence he used could not have been as successful as he was.[8]

Sir Ivan Neill also makes a shrewd assessment of the factors leading to a decline in Basil Brooke's political power base:

> Winston Churchill was Prime Minister in London during many years of Brooke's time in Government. Sir Basil's friends had great influence in government circles there. The Field Marshals, Viscount Alanbrooke, his uncle, and Viscount Alexander enjoyed a wide range of influence in the heyday of their post-war years. This influence lingered but gradually faded in the late 1950s. It was this influence he used to achieve what was best for Ulster, especially his great obsession, Ulster's security within the United Kingdom. But in the 1960s, bereft of the considerable influence of leading county gentlemen and important businessmen, and the loss of that all

important influence he enjoyed in Government circles in London, he was faced with the expectation of producing a political programme for a new age. He was unable to offer such a programme; the time had come for him to retire.[9]

Lord Brookeborough, as later generations were to know him, retired from office in March 1963 and the tributes among his fellow politicians were warm and widely echoed. But the judgement of history is likely to be harsher and to dwell on many missed opportunities and excesses in political debate. But Brookeborough was always one of Ulster's shrewdest politicians. He kept his party together during some of the most critical days in its history and helped to produce a new team of post-war Unionist leaders. Unfortunately he took an 'après moi le déluge' view of life and failed to read the new time aright. With his great authority he could have done much to bridge the North/South and the Protestant/Catholic gaps. What a different history Ulster and all of Ireland might have had if de Valera and Brookeborough in the 1950s rather than O'Neill and Lemass in the 1960s had got together – if they as senior statesmen had been willing to risk their all in a joint peacemaking mission for Ireland. They, above all others, should have been aware that time is of the essence in Irish politics, but neither Brookeborough nor de Valera seemed to sense the dangers in delay. They had failed to note the warning to those who are tardy in such matters offered in 1948 by Alan Paton in his haunting book about South Africa, *Cry, the Beloved Country*.

Alan Paton's black priest is worried about those who offer true comfort too late. And he says: 'I have one great fear in my heart, that one day when they turn to loving they will find that we have turned to hating'.[10]

'Grave and sombre words', indeed, as the author calls them. They draw attention to the unattended business confronting Irish politicians, North and South, Protestant and Catholic together, when Brookeborough's resignation in 1963 brought to an end the period of rule by Ulster's founding fathers.

REFERENCES AND NOTES

1   John A. Murphy, *Ireland in the Twentieth Century* (Gill and Macmillan, 1975, p.159).
2   Paddy Devlin, *Yes We Have No Bananas* (Blackstaff Press, 1981, p.40).
3   *Belfast News Letter*, 8 June 1921.
4   *Belfast News Letter*, 25 May 1968.
5   Harbinson, *The Ulster Unionist Party, 1882–1973*, p.142.
6   David Bleakley, *Faulkner* (Mowbray, 1974, p.40).
7   Terence O'Neill, *Autobiography* (Rupert Hart-Davis, 1972, p.40).
8   Sir Ivan Neill, Memoirs in manuscript (1994).
9   Neill, op.cit.
10 Alan Paton, *Cry, the Beloved Country* (Jonathan Cape, 1948, p.262).

PART FOUR

MESSENGERS OF CHANGE – STORMONT'S LAST PREMIERS, 1963–1972

CHAPTER 8

Terence O'Neill (1963–1969) – Great Expectations

In March 1962 the delicate balance within the Ulster Unionist Party was altered dramatically by the death of an outstanding man of action and vision, William Morrison May, Minister of Education. His death was sudden and, because he had only reached the age of fifty-three, the Province was deprived of a Unionist leader who, more than any other, had the blend of qualities needed for the political era into which he hoped to lead his party.

Morris May had a wider appeal than did any of his colleagues. He was a self-made man with an impressive business career behind him. By his forties he had amassed a large fortune; regarded as one of Ireland's most influential financiers, with good contacts in the City of London, he had the right 'image' among Unionists. His good Service record and quiet but loyal membership of the Orange Order, combined with personal charm and political drive gave him a freedom and authority denied to any of his rivals. In any community such a man would have been missed, but in a small society like Ulster the loss was a public disaster.

As the *Belfast Telegraph* put it on the night of his death: 'A Unionist couched in moderate terms and with a constant eye to the needs of the future. The feeling today that he will be extremely hard to replace is a just measure of the man.'[1]

More important, Morris May was confident of his ability to succeed Brookeborough; and, vital factors, he had the measure of Terence O'Neill and the respect of Brian Faulkner. With May as leader, all thee could have formed a successful working relationship. Nor could May have been easily passed over. He had been assured by Brookeborough that the succession would be decided at a full meeting of the Parliamentary Unionist Party. This promise was all that was required; the support of moderate Unionists, along with Faulkner's support, would have given him majority backing. Morris May never feared O'Neill as a rival, nor could his combination of wealth, talent and influence have been equalled by any other candidate from the 'Big House'. With such a candidate available O'Neill could only rank as heir presumptive. But once the massive presence of the Minister of Education was removed all was changed. Politics' oldest adage 'where there is death there is hope' had intervened again, as it had in 1953 when Major Maynard Sinclair, Minister of Finance and Lord Brookeborough's popular heir apparent, had perished in the *Princess Victoria* ferry disaster. Now in 1962 O'Neill assumed a new significance in the succession contest and began to prepare the ground.

For Faulkner the death of his friend was felt politically as well as personally. He had always enjoyed working with May and, his junior by a generation, had no intention of competing for the Premiership against him. He had expected to serve alongside his friend; the sudden tragedy caught him unprepared.

O'Neill on the other hand had long been hoping for the Premiership and the Ulster county establishment shared his hopes. So when Brookeborough resigned a year after Morris May's death, O'Neill was well placed to take over. The transfer of power was sudden and decisive. In March 1963 Brookeborough resigned, and before the Province had recovered from the sudden shock it was announced that the Governor of Northern Ireland had asked Terence O'Neill to form a new administration. The Unionist Party was particularly surprised to have been by-passed, but there was little that could be done without a major revolt. It was an Ulster version of the Westminster Douglas-Home/Butler incident; proof that Northern Ireland had its own 'magic circle'. The 'Big House' had had its way once again.

But O'Neill's method of coming to power deeply offended his parliamentary colleagues who had expected a democratic vote for the selection. Faulkner was also opposed to the method of selection and believed that it cut across the understanding which May and other Unionist leaders had established with Lord Brookeborough. Consequently, many Unionists felt that O'Neill had been imposed on the party. This greatly weakened their allegiance, as few doubted at the time that the claim of O'Neill had been given a decisive push at the right moment.

However, Terence Marne O'Neill was no newcomer to Ulster politics and had considerable Ministerial experience behind him. Born in 1914 he was the son of Captain Arthur O'Neill, MP for mid-Antrim and the first British MP to be killed in the 1914–18 War. Terence O'Neill who served in the second World War was elected to the Northern Ireland Parliament unopposed for the Bannside Co. Antrim constituency in 1946. Even Ian

Paisley, with his malicious and damaging 'O'Neill must go' campaign failed to dislodge him in the general election of 1969.

Prime Minister O'Neill got off to a good start. He was a new type Unionist and a keen student of the John F. Kennedy era. Like the Kennedys, his rise to power coincided with a developing period in TV political presentation. He recognized the media opportunities and saw to it that his 'new frontier' policies became international news.

Also, for once, the Province had a Prime Minister who was politically photogenic: a descendant on one side of the ancient O'Neill clan and on the other from Sir Arthur Chichester, with Eton and the Guards as additional guarantees of pedigree. Enough to move even the staid *Economist* to remark on his 'impeccable lineage'.

O'Neill, in fact, was the dream of the public relations industry and he was given full and generous treatment. It was of little consequence that many Ulster people were less enthusiastic; in the eyes of his admirers O'Neill could do no wrong and those who thought otherwise ran the risk of being branded as backwoodsmen. When contradictions did appear they were ignored. An O'Neill who was a member of the Orange Order was regarded as a harmless manifestation of Irish eccentricity, while lesser men who held membership faced the charge of sectarianism. Even English radicals were prepared to ignore O'Neill's upper-class conservatism; nor, much to the chagrin of local socialists, did his implacable and short-sighted opposition to the Labour movement in Northern Ireland prevent him from establishing close relationships with leading members of the British Labour Party, which he used to his advantage.

There was a further side to O'Neill's pedigree which was initially greatly to his advantage: he, more than any other candidate for the Premiership, was acceptable to many Catholics, particularly among the growing middle class. They saw him as having snatched the crown from Faulkner, who was regarded as staunchly Presbyterian and one of Brookeborough's men.

Much of this acceptance had to do with the 'Irishness' of O'Neill's lineage – an Irishness to which he often alluded when in a Catholic environment. Charles Stewart, a respected MP for Queen's University, in a congratulatory speech in the Northern Ireland Commons to mark the new appointment, spoke for many of his fellow Catholics when he welcomed the new Government in March 1963: 'It is pleasant to know that at long last we have here a Prime Minister of Northern Ireland, a person descended one way or another from Eoghan, son of Niall of the Nine Hostages, and that one of the great clans of Ulster is now represented well and truly in the chair of Prime Minister. Although he was educated at Eton, on which we commend him entirely, I only hope that his love of England will be exceeded by his love of Ireland.'[2] With Roman Catholics, simply *being* an O'Neill was an initial advantage and it enabled the Prime

Minister to make imaginative (by Unionist standards) gestures to the Catholic community on a scale never before attempted by a Unionist administration. Catholics welcomed the promised new relationships, and for a time O'Neill won support from quarters unaccustomed to voting Unionist. He became for many the acceptable face of Unionism.

Encouraged by such political windfalls, O'Neill engaged in a good deal of gesture politics in community relations. For example, in Northern Ireland terms he was a Unionist trail-blazer in showing concern for the work of Corrymeela and other bridge-building initiatives. But such outreach activity did not endear him to the reactionaries inside his own Party to whom the word 'ecumenism' was anathema. So in a sort of 'two steps forward, one step back' strategy O'Neill often seemed to be giving conflicting signals. As one of his closest advisers has recently written 'he has been subjected to mutually contradictory criticism . . . a meddler, a faint-heart'.[3]

But it was right for O'Neill to make the attempt and a pity that more of his party had not made the move earlier. O'Neill, however, laboured under the difficulty of his clan: he moved among the Roman Catholic population like some ancient lord, anxious to do the decent thing for his tenants. By his own lights he tried hard (certainly harder than any pre-vious Unionist leader) to address himself to the Catholic community, but at times they felt he failed to 'deliver'. For example, O'Neill's decision to site Ulster's second University at Coleraine, instead of Londonderry, was especially wounding to Catholics (and many Protestants as well). By so doing he refused to offer a government gift which would have gone a long way to revitalize the Derry area and to engage its people in a com-munity-binding initiative. Once again the Prime Minister had earned the rebuke, 'soft words butter no parsnips'.

Indeed, when he *did* reflect on the position of Roman Catholics in Northern Ireland, O'Neill could be revealingly offensive. In a widely quoted interview to the *Belfast Telegraph* (10 May 1969) he had this to say: 'It is frightfully hard to explain to Protestants that if you give Roman Catholics a good job and a good house, they will live like Protestants, because they will see neighbours with cars and television sets. They will refuse to have eighteen children; but if a Roman Catholic is jobless, and lives in the most ghastly hovel, he will rear eighteen children on national assistance. If you treat Roman Catholics with due consideration and kind-ness, they will live like Protestants in spite of the authoritative nature of their Church.'

As Conor Cruise O'Brien put it in a gentle but penetrating rebuke: 'It would have been even more "frightfully hard" to explain this to Catholics. Although these words were not spoken while O'Neill was still Premier, the Olympian attitude which they express was perceptible and unhelpful to his cause'.[4]

But O'Neill's Olympian attitude towards his Catholic countrymen was a factor which also caused difficulty with Protestant colleagues and followers; something less lordly is demanded by those of Planter stock with strong Scottish Presbyterian traditions. O'Neill's style of government was deeply resented and led to disagreements which weakened support for some of his most important initiatives. He ruled over Ulster like a medieval baron who genuinely believed that he knew what was best for those who lived on the estate. For a while he managed to become the most popular Ulsterman abroad and, in a series of telling 'messenger' speeches and actions, triggered off events in the Province which led to changes in the traditional political climate. But he had one great failing: he never managed to win for himself the personal support on which such high adventures must rest. This was a defect which soured relations with a series of important colleagues which in turn played havoc with his grand designs.

Even in one of his most historic gestures – the invitation of Taoiseach Sean Lemass to a meeting at Stormont Castle in January 1965 – he kept the plan secret from his Cabinet until Lemass was actually on the scene. So a very sensible and long overdue meeting lost much of its impact in the resentment caused by the exclusion of the Cabinet from a matter of high policy. Such insensitivity increasingly isolated O'Neill from colleagues on whom he ultimately depended and should have won over.

Fortunately O'Neill had the good sense to surround himself with a circle of highly experienced civil servants who protected him as best they could – and perhaps too much. Two in particular, Jim Malley and Ken Bloomfield, did most of the 'marketing' of their master. O'Neill in his autobiography acknowledged his good fortune: 'Seldom has a minister been better served than I was by these two men'.[5] Bloomfield explained the system in a frank and very readable recent memoir, *Stormont in Crisis*: 'Malley became known as the Prime Minister's "leg-man" and intimate, and was constantly on the telephone, either at the office or at home, in his master's cause. My own role was to be the word-spinner and ideas man of the Castle'. In John F. Kennedy-era language, they were known as the 'Presidential aides': 'To the extent that this was so, Bateman and Black (top civil servants) played the role of Dean Rusk, Malley was Larry O'-Brien and I was Ted Sorensen'.[6]

This is a revealing passage and takes us to the heart of a problem which those of us who were members of the Stormont Parliament realized all too clearly in O'Neill's time – the Prime Minister of Northern Ireland was not at home with the parliamentary system. Too often his approach was Presidential – he needed more reminding by his civil service that remoteness from colleagues was highly dangerous in the intimate politics of a deeply divided Province. Even an O'Neill could not afford to 'go it alone'.

I often sympathized with Unionist MPs who felt ignored by their leader and for whom he had little regard. A highly respected member of the

Commons once said to me: 'Why is it that the PM when he passes me in the Lobby always forgets my name – and, worse still, often says, "Good-day Gerry" ', confusing him with Republican Socialist MP Gerry Fitt (later Lord Fitt), then a Stormont MP! Oddly enough, this most enigmatic of premiers sometimes felt more at home with the Opposition and occasionally took their advice. I remember once suggesting that trade union leaders should be used more often in public appointments. He took the hint and many excellent postings were made. Equally, he responded to suggestions that he should make more contact with local community relations groups and made many ecumenical visits.

But as the sixties drew to a close Ulster's fourth prime minister was increasingly isolated. Much of his grand design was in tatters – Camelot it was not. The reform programmes failed to take off because they so often lacked the authority of firm parliamentary backing; nor could even the best scripts of his chosen civil servants protect O'Neill at the Dispatch Box. To those of us who faced him from the Opposition benches he seemed a harassed and lonely figure. Cross-examination by Labour and Independent members was fair enough, but too often the real embarrassment came from those behind him; their taunts and wrecking tactics were clearly hard to bear. Occasionally Terence O'Neill glanced over his shoulder in despair. When he did, I was sure he often recalled the utterance of one of his famous countrymen, Wellington: 'I don't know what effect these men will have upon the enemy, but, by God, they terrify me'.

Without a united parliamentary party behind him and with increasing violence on the streets, O'Neill began more and more a direct appeal to the people of Northern Ireland. But it was too late. After an apparent election triumph in 1965 things began to go seriously wrong as 'fifty-year' celebrations began to loom up. For each tradition, memories of 1916 had special meaning; a potential was developed for flash-point confrontations across a divided community. To add to his torment he had to contend with reactionary and destabilizing forces represented by the rising fortunes of Ian Paisley and Bernadette Devlin, each of whom was eventually elected to Westminster. Differing in politics but, as far as the prime minister was concerned, they shared a common cause: 'O'Neill must go'. The fusion of their raucous propaganda produced a devastating lethal mixture.

When O'Neill did decide to go his decision was swift and final. In a famous 'Crossroads' broadcast, which received world coverage in December 1968, he spoke of his five years' effort 'to heal some of the deep divisions in our community' and warned against the growing civil disorder which had put the Province 'on the brink of chaos'. He appealed to the Civil Rights Movement to call their people off the streets so that new legislation would have a chance to improve basic community relations. And he warned 'if you want a separate, inward-looking, selfish and divided Ulster then you must seek for others to lead you along that road, for I cannot and will not do it'.[7]

Five months later this most patrician of Ulster leaders carried out his threat and laid down 'what had increasingly become totally impossible burdens'. Sadly for Ulster, he was unable to agree that the succession should go to Brian Faulkner who was widely expected to succeed. But long-felt grievances prevailed. O'Neill decided to intervene in the leadership election and was delighted to see that his vote when cast gave Faulkner's rival a majority of one. In his memoirs he explains simply: 'I couldn't have brought myself to vote for the man who had been trying to bring me down for six years. It was as simple as that.'[8]

But there was more to it than that. It was a tragic fact that these two complex and talented men had an extraordinarily low level of tolerance for each other – in British terms a bit like Hugh Gaitskill and Aneuran Bevan. O'Neill was all that Faulkner was not and did not wish to be: Eton, the Guards and Anglican. Faulkner, for his part, was only 'in trade' as far as the landed aristocracy were concerned – someone who, in their eyes, did not know his proper place. The two men even disagreed on their attitude to their old leader. Faulkner was deeply loyal to Brookeborough and regarded him as 'one of Ulster's greatest leaders and a fine man to serve under'; O'Neill's subsequent comments on the veteran Unionist were devastatingly critical and hurtful.

Indeed, O'Neill's aloofness cost him many friends and at times he could have done with some of Brookeborough's country charm. Unfortunately he was in many ways a prisoner of the aristocratic remoteness associated with the O'Neill line. It was at once his greatest asset and heaviest liability – good for foreign consumption, but difficult to retail at home.

Had they come together they would have made a formidable team. Brian Faulkner seems to have regretted the rift. In his autobiography, published posthumously after his tragically early death, Faulkner makes the comment: 'Terence O'Neill was a hardworking Prime Minister who had much to contribute to Northern Ireland. Had we been able to work together better I think we would have made a strong team for the good of Northern Ireland. But I do not think he ever felt really at home in Ulster politics. His personal remoteness made it difficult for him to lead his Party along new and difficult paths at a very crucial point in the Province's history.' Once again the suggestion of great expectations, with a failure to deliver.[9]

But there was a positive side to the O'Neill contribution which classifies him as a 'messenger of change' – one of the special people central to the theme of this book. These 'messengers', a courageous minority, have been concerned to create an agenda around which Ulster people, Protestant and Catholic together, can congregate in fellowship. By such standards, Terence O'Neill earns a significant place in the political history of his time. He had the courage to face up to the forces of sectarianism which, from all sides, closed in upon him. And he was proud to proclaim that he 'had won the trust of the Catholics as no Prime Minister had ever been able to do, but was unable to restore to them the rights which small-minded men had removed from them during the first few years of Northern Ireland's existence'.[10] By such affirmations O'Neill placed reconciliation at the centre of Ulster's political agenda.

Equally, even at a time when democratic structures were seeming to fail and the rule of law was being recklessly threatened, his appeal for a 'new politics' stimulated fresh political thinking provincewide. As a result, the Unionist Party gained new members (many of them Catholics); nationalists in 1970 were reinvigorated by the emergence of the Social Democratic and Labour Party which provided a constitutional outlet for the energies of a new generation of radical young Catholics; and, even more significant, in 1969 the New Ulster Movement was formed as a pressure group to promote moderation and non-sectarian politics. Later the NUM developed into the Alliance Party of Northern Ireland, as a means of uniting Protestants and Catholics on a platform of agreed radical policies. Taking the strategically sound decision to concentrate on Northern Ireland's community problems, and with a non-sectarian membership at all levels, the new-look Alliance Party attracted and virtually monopolized the centre vote previously garnered by other moderate groups of longer lineage. A particular casualty was the trade union-supported Northern Ireland Labour Party (once the sister party of the British Labour Party) which even as late as 1970 (but before PR) had won 12.6 per cent of the vote in the General Election.

By stimulating such developments in the body politic, Terence O'Neill had done much to preserve the democratic party political fabric which would be required to build the New Ulster and Agreed Ireland which lay at the centre of much of his thinking.

But in May 1969 when O'Neill left Northern Ireland, there were no such reflections or consolations. He was still in the prime of life and, politically and provincewide, he had a loyal cross-community following. For the many who had flocked to support this true son of the 'Big House' and the new Unionism he advocated so eloquently, his sudden resignation and departure for England was a traumatic experience. It was a 'Flight of the Earls' all over again; his followers were left stunned and leaderless. For those who stood to gain politically from the downfall, or who seemed involved in that downfall, there was no love. Many grieving O'Neillites were among the most influential people in the Province; for a time their pursuit of those deemed guilty was unrelenting and damaging.

The 'Big House' was down but not yet out; it made one more attempt to fight back.

REFERENCES AND NOTES

1 *Belfast Telegraph*, 2 March 1962.
2 David Bleakley, *Faulkner* (Mowbray, 1974, p.69).
3 Ken Bloomfield, *Stormont in Crisis* (Blackstaff Press, 1994, p.76).
4 Conor Cruise O'Brien, *States of Ireland* (Hutchinson, 1972, p.170).
5 O'Neill, *Autobiography* (Rupert Hart-Davis, 1972, p.35).
6 Bloomfield, op.cit., p.75.
7 O'Neill, op.cit., p.145.
8 O'Neill, *ibid.*, 129.
9 Brian Faulkner, *Memoirs of a Statesman* (Weidenfeld and Nicolson, 1978, p.53).
10 O'Neill, op.cit., p.129.

CHAPTER 9

James Chichester-Clarke (1969–1971) – Fall of the 'Big House'

TERENCE O'NEILL'S RESIGNATION signalled the end of 'Big House' rule in Northern Ireland – from then on the landed aristocracy would have to earn their public 'keep' by engaging in the democratic rough and tumble of twentieth-century political debate. Initially, the departure of O'Neill seemed likely to open the way for Brian Faulkner, the manufacturer's son, who was a vivid reminder that things would never be the same again in Ulster politics. But before this new fact of life sank in there was to be an unexpected period of waiting imposed by Faulkner's opponents.

In a bitterly contested election, it was decided (by a very narrow margin) to call in a 'safe man' to unite the party and to engage in damage limitation. For Faulkner it was the fate of America's Lyndon Johnson all over again. The hand that killed John F. Kennedy may have been that of Lee Harvey Oswald, but it was the accession and the presence of L.B.J. that became the constant reminder of what had gone before. Faulkner would be required to wait – perhaps for ever, was the hope of many O'Neillites.

James Chichester-Clarke had an unenviable task, but he came to his new post with many advantages. Like his predecessor, he had solid connections among the Unionist elite. Born in 1923, he too was educated at Eton and had served in the Irish Guards. On leaving the Army he was returned unopposed for the safe Stormont seat of South Derry, held previously by his father and his grandmother – the Irish version of a 'pocket borough', of which there have been many, both North and South.

So, for those who wished to continue in a pattern-as-before-style the member for South Derry seemed a natural 'safe hands' choice. But all concerned were to be greatly surprised: James Chichester-Clarke may have seemed destined for an unexciting short term of office, but in his brisk reign of twenty-two months 'Northern Ireland in general, and the Unionist Party in particular, underwent a revolution'.[1] That assessment by the leading historian of the Ulster Unionist Party, John F. Harbinson, is widely endorsed by politicians who were involved in the process.

It was not that the new Prime Minister was revolutionary in intent; what mattered was the revolutionary effect of some of his policies. Most momentous was the decision in August 1969 to call on the British Government to involve the Army in the maintenance of law and order in the Province. The transfer of this devolved power from Belfast to London signalled a dramatic reduction in the authority of the Stormont Government and introduced a system of power- and responsibility-sharing between Belfast and London of great constitutional significance. The long-standing convention of non-intervention in Northern Ireland matters by Westminster was swept away, and relationship questions which had lain dormant for years were placed firmly on the table for discussion. The 'quiet man' of Ulster politics had created a whole new constitutional agenda after only five months in office; no one, not even Harold Wilson, was prepared for the event. From August 1969, when the troops were employed in their peacekeeping and peacemaking duties, the question of where power lay in Northern Ireland was to concern and perplex a long line of Westminster and North Irish politicians. For all, it proved a sobering experience.

The process of dividing powers started gently enough. When in 1969 British troops took over their new role in Northern Ireland they were generally well received and it was widely believed, and hoped, that their presence would not be required for long. But others, notably Home Secretary James Callaghan and some of his closest military advisers, were not so sure.

However, Callaghan, who brought dedication and enthusiasm to his task, was a reassuring presence. His commitment was impressive. As he wrote later: 'Certainly in simple human terms it was the most meaningful experience of my life . . . '.[2] (This sentiment was later echoed by Merlyn Rees, another Labour Minister with a deep sense of commitment: 'I would not have wanted any other job'.)[3] Callaghan was very much his own man and he was also left very much on his own. His colleagues were on holiday in August 1969 and were, in any case, more likely than not to regard Ireland as a graveyard for British politicians. Callaghan knew better; well versed in the local scene and with many trade union and Labour contacts, he set out to exercise real authority and 'to do it quickly or be swamped'.[4] His stamp of authority and direction was historic in consequence: he established a *modus operandi* which has pointed the way for later Secretaries of State who have built on his pioneer intervention.

Chichester-Clarke did not plan for this development, and certainly did not foresee the full implications, but deep down he and his party undoubtedly realized that by seeking the direct intervention of the British Army they were abrogating their responsibility for the preservation of law and order as enacted by Act of Parliament. It was a high-risk policy and required a delicate balance-of-powers exercise between London and Belfast. But very soon the Government of Chichester-Clarke was made aware of the implications of the new arrangements: there could be no blank cheque from London. Something for something would be required. In particular, it was made clear by Callaghan that a reform programme would have to be undertaken by the Northern Ireland Government which would guarantee parity of esteem between citizens inside Northern Ireland and between Northern Ireland and the rest of the United Kingdom. More long-term in its implications, there was a recognition that the harmonization of Stormont/Westminster relations would require the establishment of a system of joint working parties, with London civil servants seconded to Northern Ireland to coordinate the consultative process. For civil servants the phrase 'you cannot serve two masters' took on fresh meaning! Some commentators at the time, particularly the SDLP's Austin Currie, believed that the coming of the troops and the suspension of Stormont should have been a combined operation, so depriving the IRA of their 'Stormont must go' campaign slogan.

But the British Government had no such finely tuned policies. As James Callaghan has subsequently recorded, it was very much a case of living from hand to mouth where policy was concerned. As well, he had to get used to the special language of Irish politics – sometimes hilariously so, as when he once reminded Mr Paisley that 'we are all the children of God' only to be rebuffed by the Reverend Ian: 'No we are not, Mr Callaghan. We are all the children of Wrath'.[5]

But the British Home Secretary was more than a match for Unionist politicians and the many others who came his way. He let the press know that he wanted to be a catalyst and did not want Britain to get more embroiled in Northern Ireland than it had to. But he also made it clear that there was a mailed fist in reserve: if Stormont should be incapable of functioning and if law and order were to break down completely then the British Government would be ready, though reluctant, to apply emergency contingency powers to assert its authority.

Such an assertion of Westminster authority was not offensive to Prime Minister Chichester-Clarke, whose recognition of Westminster supremacy was complete and unambiguous. However, in the deteriorating security situation, his cooperation with Downing Street did not endear him to the Stormont members on whom he depended. It was an invidious position for a man who placed honour and service high in his priorities. Especially hard to bear was the suggestion that Westminster had him on a string. Particularly wounding was an August 1969 article in the prestigious *Spectator*. Under the heading 'Ulster finds her Husak', Chichester-Clarke was compared with Husak, who had replaced the more patriotic Dubcek, in Czechoslovakia. The conclusion was offered: 'Certainly there is no need to abolish Stormont and revert to direct Westminster rule so long as Major Chichester-Clarke is prepared to play Husak to Whitehall's Kremlin . . . all that can be done now is to reaffirm that the border is a permanency . . . and then to hope that within this secure context, the forces of reason will, gradually, once more begin to prevail over those of unreason.'[6]

But *Spectator* readers' time is not Ulster people's time; the forces of reason were not to prevail in the period allotted to Ulster's fifth prime minister.

The reform programme which he was required to implement was certainly got underway and an impressive infrastructure was created. Reforms to do with policing, local government, community relations, housing allocation, ombudsman services and a Prevention of Incitement to Hatred Act were now in the pipeline. Indeed, many in Whitehall felt that such reforms would speedily transform the situation. But on home ground things were different. Neither the anarchist student 'left' nor the reactionary Unionist 'right' was impressed; nor did they cease their reckless 'Chichester-Clarke must go' campaign. Once again the truth of Eisenhower's aphorism became apparent: 'You can't think straight when you're frightened stiff'.[7] So it was in early-1970s Northern Ireland. With the increase in paramilitary activity and the new threat represented by the creation of the Provisional IRA there was a swift and frightening deterioration in the security situation. Those who worked for better community relations were put under further strains as sectarian violence and horrendous murders intensified. For such a decline Chichester-Clarke was, increasingly, held personally responsible. Furthermore, his fragile parliamentary majority had been dramatically weakened by the election in April 1970 of two prominent and vociferous Protestant Unionists – Ian Paisley (in Terence O'Neill's former seat) and William Beattie for South Antrim. In a small Commons of fifty-two seats such an outcome represented a considerable rebuff to the Prime Minister – indeed, the result was described by experts as 'probably the most vital in the history of the Stormont House of Commons'.[8]

Increasingly for Chichester-Clarke the question was: 'When are you going to do something about law and order?' The Prime Minister hoped to make his reform programme a rallying point for a divided and uneasy Province but his appeals went unheard – Parliament and supporters in the country wanted more action on security. In desperation Chichester-Clarke turned to Westminster with a last demand for a greatly increased military presence. As he pointed out, he had to quell the violence if his reforms were to be given a chance. These overtures were unsuccessful and in a resignation, which an alarmed British Government tried hard to prevent, he left office disillusioned but never publicly bitter.

Many in Northern Ireland felt that James Chichester-Clarke deserved better from his masters at Westminster. During his premiership, major reform programmes were got through Parliament at a rate never before known in Stormont's history – all against a background of a security crisis. These were, in themselves, significant developments and, no doubt, Chichester-Clarke would wish to be remembered for them. But historically he will always be associated with the decision in August 1969 to call upon the British Government for military assistance. He had signalled a dramatic change in direction which could not be ignored. Gladstone's *cri de coeur* comes to mind: 'Just when you begin to understand the Irish Question they change the question'.

By his action in 1969 and his willingness to cooperate with the processes of joint sovereignty between Belfast and London, Chichester-Clarke had made a 'messenger' contribution to Ulster politics. He had dramatically changed the question – wisely he concluded that it was time for another to search for an answer.

In March 1971 this last prime minister from Ulster's 'Big House' stock felt able to resign with honour and return to the gentler cares of his extensive estate. He and his successor parted on good terms and with mutual respect, each aware of what was at stake in the governance of Northern Ireland.

REFERENCES AND NOTES

1   Harbinson, *The Ulster Unionist Party, 1882–1973* (Blackstaff Press, 1973, p.155).
2   James Callaghan, *A House Divided* (Collins, 1973, p.70).
3   Merlyn Rees, *Northern Ireland – a Personal Perspective* (Methuen, 1985, p.35).
4   Callaghan, op.cit., p.70.
5   *Ibid.*, p.82.
6   Paul Bew and Gordon Gillespie, *Chronology of the Troubles, 1968–1993* (Gill and Macmillan, p.21).
7   *Ibid.*, p.26.
8   *Ibid.*

CHAPTER 10

Brian Faulkner (1971–1972) – Redefining Unionism

PUBLIC OPINION was on the side of Brian Faulkner in 1971. Many had sympathized with him when he had been outvoted by Chichester-Clarke's supporters in 1969 and the sympathy had grown as, in the role of Deputy Prime Minister, he had more and more shouldered the full burden of leadership. His succession, when it came, seemed to many to be overdue, and to most it was a just reward for years of persistent application.

Born in 1921 into a wealthy Co. Down manufacturing family, Faulkner was educated in Armagh and Dublin. The latter schooling was important, giving him an invaluable experience of life in the South of Ireland and personal connections which he always valued. Entering Parliament for East Down in 1949, he was soon 'spotted' by Lord Brookeborough and given swift promotion in party ranks. Unfortunately for Faulkner's later reputation, he early on became involved in security issues, particularly so following his first Cabinet appointment to Home Affairs. In this Department he became known as the administrator of the controversial Special Powers Act and the even more contentious practice of internment, which was used against the IRA in their campaign in the 1950s. Not until 1963, when he was appointed Minister of Commerce, did Brian Faulkner's preference and flair for industrial development become apparent – from then, until his departure from Stormont, he was the Government's greatest job promoter and did much to transform the industrial base of the Province.

When Faulkner became Prime Minister in March 1971, he took over at a desperate moment in the life of Northern Ireland, but in a typical display of determination he began to grasp whatever advantages were available in the new situation. He had waited a long time for the Premiership and, as with others who achieved top office, the attitudes adopted in the climb began to give way to a political lifestyle needed to consolidate the position reached and designed to make full use of the new opportunities. As it happened, the tenure in office of Ulster's sixth and last Premier was to be a shortest-ever (one year and one day), but in long-term effect it overshadowed those of his predecessors in constitutional and historical significance. Terence O'Neill's career, for instance, was one of frustrated promise, during which he had offered the Ulster people a revolution of rising expectations; but it was Faulkner, his greatest rival, who faced up to the infinitely more difficult task of ensuring legislative change which gave effect to the 'new frontier' policies so eloquently proclaimed by O'Neill.

Though the public gave Faulkner a ready welcome, the professional politicians were more cautious. From Social Democratic Labour Party leader, Mr Gerry Fitt, came the charge that the new government lacked 'credibility'. Mr John Hume agreed with this and accused Faulkner of being party to 'a pretence and charade of democracy'. The new Premier fared no better at the hands of right-wing Unionists. For Ian Paisley's *Protestant Telegraph* it was recent history that mattered most: 'We remember him for his pushing through the reform programme, including the Housing Executive Bill. We remember him for his enthusiasm for cross-border talks. We know that he has had secret talks with Cardinal Conway. That should please the Orange brethren. We know of his business interests in the South of Ireland. Faulkner's declared policies are but the sugar coating of a bitter pill, and during the next few weeks the real, the aggressive, the dictatorial Faulkner will emerge, but he could be Ulster's shortest reigning Prime Minister, as we will not tolerate any further erosion of our standards and principles.' Buffeted equally by both sides, not for the first time, Faulkner must have thought 'you can't win!'[1]

But the opinion of the politicians was not representative, and most Ulster people were prepared to give the new administration a fair trial. It was widely realized that time was running out for the Province and that a 'last chance' Prime Minister had arrived.

The new Premier soon displayed his outstanding resilience and an ability to fight his way out of a difficult corner. Everything began to seem possible as he began to break entirely new ground – new by the conservative standards associated with traditional Unionist leadership.

Signs of a special brand of Faulkner Unionism appeared in his approach to Cabinet-building. Unlike his predecessors, he was prepared to step outside the traditional framework of Ulster politics. Realizing that official Unionist custom and practice was no longer sufficient for the immediate crisis, Faulkner declared that in creating his government he sought to develop 'not a rigid or doctrinaire administration representative of any single opinion or outlook, but a broadly-based government, which brings together men who stand united in the interests of the country'. So, in the new Cabinet the broadest possible spectrum of Unionism was represented. Harry West, sacked by O'Neill, returned to his beloved Ministry of Agriculture to do an excellent job for his farmers, while Robin Baillie (a Bow Group type, who a few years later joined the Alliance Party) came in as Minister of Commerce and as a strong supporter of the EEC. Other members who represented various shades of Unionism joined the new team. By all accounts it was a shrewd balance though, at the same time, it attracted a cross-section of reservations from many who were surprised by the new style and wondered what it represented.

But Faulkner in the construction of his first Cabinet had another surprise in store – he decided to broaden the party political basis of his government. Down the years the Unionist Party had been criticized for its monopoly of power; Faulkner decided to innovate. In a surprise move, he sought the assistance of his political opponents, the Labour Party. A member of the Northern Ireland Labour Party (the present writer) was invited to become Minister of Community Relations in the new government and to accept a seat in the Cabinet. In Ulster terms it was an unprecedented event.

Faulkner's approach in making this appointment was typical of his workmanlike style. On the day in question I was lecturing at the Methodist College, Belfast, and was interrupted by a telephone call from Robert Ramsey, the Prime Minister's Secretary. Could I come to Stormont Castle at 10.15 a.m.? Mr Faulkner had some important business to discuss. There was, in fact, nothing unusual about such a call: those of us involved in peacemaking were often involved in such visits. But this time it was different. The Prime Minister came to the point straight away. He had been asked by the Governor to form a new government and was anxious to construct a Cabinet which would have broadly-based community support. The country must be got going again, the reform programme had to be carried through, and other reforms would follow as stability was established. We needed to make a united effort – would I help?

At that time I had recently returned from a two-year tour of service in Kirukoni College, Julius Nyerere's leadership training centre in Tanzania, and so I was not a Member of Parliament. Here again the Prime Minister was prepared. There was no problem – the Constitution was very flexible: I could be sworn in as a Privy Councillor and on that basis would be able to serve in Cabinet for at least a six-month period. Would I join on this basis as Minister of Community Relations? There would be no 'strings' and no interference with my Labour or trade union membership obligations (undertakings honoured at all times). Could I give my answer by one o'clock?

In that manner Brian Faulkner made what was a mould-breaking innovation, opening up a new pattern for inner-party appointments to government in Northern Ireland. At a luncheon later in the day, attended by Jim Callaghan (who that evening gave generous support on TV), I indicated my acceptance. A new Minister of Community Relations had been appointed to the Northern Ireland Government and a first-ever member of the Labour Party had been admitted to the Cabinet of the Province.

The decision to serve in Faulkner's government was, initially, a lonely one. In 1971 the concept of community government in Northern Ireland was new and was not popular in any of the major political parties in Parliament. But, as a life-long pacifist and peacemaker, I had no doubts. Since 1969 the erosion of the social and political structure indicated all too clearly that political tribalism based on sectarian confrontation had had its day – that some form of community power-sharing (and, more important, responsibility-sharing) would have to take its place. Someday, somehow, the people of Northern Ireland had to make a start. By appointing a Cabinet Minister from outside the Unionist Party, Brian Faulkner had shown a willingness to move towards a power-sharing model of government, alien to all previous Unionist leaders.

Some Unionists objected to the Prime Minister's decision, but it was soon evident that public opinion at home and wider afield applauded his initiative. Not all appreciated the long-term political significance of a non-Unionist appointment, but the general sense was one of agreeing that this was an idea whose time had come. From both sides of Westminster came messages of congratulations, with Edward Heath being especially helpful; so, too, was Jack Lynch, the Taoiseach in the Irish Republic: 'In the special circumstances that exist in the North it is a very good idea'.

Cross-community support for Faulkner's new initiative was equally marked. From the Roman Catholic Archbishop came congratulations; as well, there were messages of support from other Irish church bodies; and I had generous best wishes from the Conference of European Churches and the World Council of Churches, in which I represented Ireland. Particularly appreciated was a personal letter from Archbishop Michael Ramsey conveying good wishes from Lambeth Palace on the night of my appointment: 'My very best wishes in the new task which you are under-taking. Your colleagues in the Anglican Consultative Council will be proud that this has fallen to you and many good wishes and prayers will surround you.' Such support was encouraging and indicative of the fund of international goodwill which accompanies the Irish in their search for peace.

The most searching comment on Faulkner's initiative came in a letter from Brian Walker, founder of the influential cross-community New Ulster Movement and Director of Oxfam. Brian saw the development as mould-breaking and as being at one with all the Movement had been trying to achieve for years: 'It opens a door to new opportunities for the whole community to free itself from the past.' This noted observer con-cluded: 'I felt the same kind of elation in 1966 when NUM organised the

celebrated Corrymeela Conference which allowed Unionist Premier
O'Neill to speak on our basic problems to a joint Catholic-Protestant
audience – for the first time.'

Subsequent developments have confirmed this judgement and have
made notions of sharing in government more commonplace. But in the
Ulster of 1971 Faulkner was ahead of his time. By having the courage to
make the offer, and in securing a positive response from a representative
of the Labour movement, the Premier had made a first contribution to
the concept of partnership in government; he had created a precedent
which made future constitutional thinking along similar lines easier to
develop. Nor was the offer a once-for-all gesture on Faulkner's part. By
his decision later in 1971 to appoint Dr G. B. Newe, a leading Roman
Catholic layman, to his Cabinet he showed that he was willing to pursue
the idea further and more effectively than any other Unionist leader. On
another occasion he also approached a leading trade union official (a non-
Unionist) to join the government.

In March 1971, Faulkner, never inclined to produce a theory to explain
his actions, gave no indication that he was deliberately experimenting with
new forms of government, but it was a sound instinct that made him
aware of the need to reach out for assistance beyond the Ulster Unionist
Party. In our regular discussions this was a recurring theme. Towards the
end of his Premiership he began to talk more openly about his hopes for
a broadening of the base of power and for a party membership that was
non-sectarian. As he put it to the Commons (3 November 1971): 'I look
forward to the day when my Unionist colleagues on this Front Bench will
be Protestant and Catholic, and no one will even think it worthy of
comment. Neither Unionist nor Ulster will survive in the long run if we
take any other course.' Words of enduring relevance.

Other 'sacred cows' of Unionism were challenged by Ulster's last Prime
Minister. Early in his ministry, he promised 'to serve all the people of
Northern Ireland' and stressed his determination to make 'no distinction
between Protestant and Roman Catholic'. In subsequent months this
theme became a major element in official statements.

Faulkner's second new theme concerned relations inside Parliament.
Here he stressed that Parliament belonged to all the Members (a far cry
from the old-fashioned Unionist Party days of 'a Protestant Parliament for
a Protestant people'). In particular, he saw a key role for the Opposition.
He offered to have discussions with Mr Fitt, leader of the largest opposition group, so as to enable the House to reach an agreed approach on
matters of common concern. Little attention was paid to these overtures,
but seeds were being sown which would blossom at the Darlington and
Sunningdale constitutional conferences some months and many crises
later. The appeal was rounded-off with a personal hope, expressed so
consistently down the years, that the government 'should be judged on

their record, on what they actually do, rather than on fanciful speculation about what they might do'.

Faulkner did not have much time in his single year of office to accumulate many legislative achievements, but even in the short time available a new framework of ideas was discernible. In developing this framework he did not take up a doctrinaire position, either Unionist or Conservative, and he managed to get Cabinet agreement for projects which, in any other period in the history of the Province, might well have caused a split in the administration. Very rarely did the Cabinet get into doctrinal dispute; the times were too pressing for other than practical propositions. Indeed, the Northern Irish, generally, are more pragmatic about practical politics than their English counterparts and are often astonished and dismayed by the ideological social and economic policies pursued by Direct Rule Ministers and their mandarins from Whitehall.

In another sensitive area of community relations – fair employment policies – Faulkner proved a pioneer. Catholics had long demonstrated that they were discriminated against where job allocation was concerned. The new Prime Minister became the first Unionist to legislate against the practice. A law was passed debarring from public contracts any firm which practised religious discrimination in the performance of the contract. This move was an important lead to the rest of industry, and the private sector took steps to introduce similar safeguards. A few years earlier, such an agreement would have ranked as front-page material and as the mark of an enlightened administration, but in the mood of late 1971 it could not compete with more sombre news.

It was, in fact, Faulkner's misfortune that some of his most liberal initiatives had to be undertaken at a time when they were overshadowed by community tensions of greater public concern. Such, in particular, became the fate of his most important and final initiative, before Direct Rule was imposed by Westminster – he offered a new system of government at Stormont, based on inter-party committees of the House of Commons.

The offer was made in the middle of a remarkable speech delivered on the afternoon of 22 June 1971. The speech marked a turning point in Faulkner's thinking and spelt out in detail the new philosophy at which he had hinted in his March speech on the Address. The occasion was well chosen. It was the fiftieth anniversary of the opening of the first Parliament of Northern Ireland. Ulster people, despite their troubles, were in festive mood and, Protestant and Catholic together, were aware that in fifty years they had established something of a common destiny. A province-wide Festival was taking place and, miraculously, even the bombers left the colourful exhibition halls and happy community events alone. With the aid of the poets, painters and playwrights of the Province, Planter and Gael, the Ulster people together for a few Golden Jubilee weeks realized with a shy surprise that there was, deep down, a common heritage to be enjoyed and praised. As Minister of Community Relations I welcomed this feeling of oneness and pointed to its fuller significance.

Much of this sense of new discovery was reflected in the Prime Minister's speech to the Commons. After pointing briefly to what he described as 'the most comprehensive programme of structural and other changes ever undertaken in Northern Ireland' he left the 'bricks and mortar' of progress and proceeded to startle the House by turning to questions concerning the fundamental nature of the Ulster community. With a reminder that all sides had fallen short in the past half-century, he proceeded to proclaim his faith in the possibility of a United Ulster where no false distinction would be drawn between citizen and citizen. He frankly admitted his own mistakes and those of his party and suggested that the time had come for radical changes in attitudes. He challenged the members to follow him in an entirely new effort to 'summon up new reserves of generosity and imagination', and went on to point out the possibilities inherent in the regional institutions of Northern Ireland, provided they could lay aside the inter-communal exchanges which had become 'increasingly bitter and sterile'.

Faulkner then proposed to a startled and increasingly rapt House that the government would give a new lead which would enable all – Protestant and Catholic together – to participate more fully in the work of government. He offered a system of functional committees of the House in which some of the most powerful posts of Chairman would go to members of the opposition. These committees would be able to contribute to policy formation and would probe the executive functions of ministries and other agencies of government. All committees would be properly serviced and special allowances would be paid to members involved. In this way, he suggested, government and opposition alike would be involved more closely in the running of the State. He hoped that such a system would eliminate some of the inevitable frustrations and tensions associated with permanent opposition.

In the Northern Ireland setting such proposals represented a sea-change in approach and the statement was regarded as such by politicians and public alike.

But more was to follow. Faulkner also took up a point which he had mentioned in passing in an earlier speech to the House – inter-party discussions. The times were serious and he believed that partisan conflict must be excluded as far as possible from the political arena. He did not believe that the aspirations of members on either side were as far apart as public speechmaking might suggest. He wondered, therefore, if the needs of the country did not justify a serious attempt 'to bring the various political interests represented together for frank and wide-ranging discussions'. His conditions for such discussions revealed the new dimension in which he was working. There would have to be a full spectrum of views; talks would be open-ended; and while constitutional changes would not be on the agenda neither would any of the participants be expected 'in any way to derogate' from nationalist policies. He concluded by suggesting that the central purpose of the discussions should concern the common ground of restoring peace and stability and resuming social and economic advantages.

In the context of his time and party affiliation, Faulkner had made a remarkable gesture. Even his most severe critics recognized the magnitude of what he was saying and his proposals were listened to without interruption. When he had finished, the 'Hear, hears' in the House were many-sided and enthusiastic. It was a keynote occasion and members recognized it as such; more than two decades later the speech repays reading.

From Gerry Fitt, Leader of the Opposition, came a welcome for the promise 'to try new projects and to take a different line from that taken over the past fifty years'. He promised that if the Prime Minister put his words into action then he would have the cooperation of the Opposition. Labour spokesman, Vivian Simpson, regarded the contribution as 'a very brilliant speech' and welcomed the 'genuine desire to share Parliamentary responsibility with the Opposition'. He promised the full support of the Labour movement. Austin Currie, from the SDLP, and one of the strongest critics of the government, had no doubts either. For him, the debate had been one of the best of its kind since his coming to the House: 'The Prime Minister is well aware that it is not very often I compliment him in public, or in private for that matter, but I intend to do so on this occasion. I think it was his contribution to this debate which encouraged other members to contribute good speeches. He raised the tone of the debate and the result was that a number of other members attempted to do the same thing.' Currie also promised that his side would be prepared to play a part in the House, as of right: 'We do not need to be invited to play our part. We are prepared to do so as members of this House. We recognise what the Prime Minister asked us to recognise, namely that participation involves accepting burdens as well as enjoying advantages. We are quite prepared to accept those burdens.' Coming from one of the SDLP's clearest thinkers, this was praise indeed and contained significant gestures.

All that was needed to make Faulkner's triumph complete was a word of congratulation from Mr Paddy Devlin, for long his most turbulent opponent. Devlin, too, had been won over and was generous in his tribute: 'Let me turn to the Prime Minister's proposals. I am pleased to welcome the proposals in the speech. They showed plenty of imagination. It was his best hour since I came into the House. If the promise that is contained in those proposals is implemented we will possibly get over the bad period towards which we are heading as a result of trouble on the streets. The Prime Minister has given hon. members, and indirectly those outside, an opportunity to share in decision-making on a far greater scale than up to now.'

When Faulkner came to reply to the debate he was visibly moved by the volume of praise which his new approach had evoked. Altogether, it was a new experience and one he could not fail to notice. He had released new ideas on to the local political scene and had discovered that his opponents were willing to listen; he had also discovered that beyond the bounds of traditional Unionism there was undiscovered country which was attractive to explore. He had begun to sense a new dimension; the 'Ulster Unionist' was beginning to give way to the 'United Ulsterman'. It was an hour of unusual glory; he basked deservedly in it.[2]

So far, 1971 had been something of an *annus mirabilis* for Northern Ireland's last Prime Minister. The ideas enunciated by Faulkner had – in quality, daring and application – far outreached those of any of his five predecessors. But if June 1971 was Faulkner's finest moment in the House it was also the prelude to his most difficult period of trial and isolation. Increased violence on the streets of Northern Ireland in the summer of 1971 and pressure from Dublin-based politicians eroded political confidence; soon all effective dialogue ended. In July the SDLP decided to intensify their campaign against Stormont and withdrew from the Assembly to set up a rival body of their own. The grand design for the future of government machinery in the Province got lost in the bitterness which followed. In the long hot summer the people of Northern Ireland, and the politicians with them; gradually lost sight of new schemes for government as they tried desperately to maintain any form of government at all in the face of a terrorist campaign which threatened the whole fabric of their lives. For most, the issues were too stark to allow time for erudite political discussion – survival was all that mattered. More and more Faulkner began to prepare for the Doomsday position which, he believed, was fast approaching.

Cabinet colleagues saw less and less of the Prime Minister as during the long hot summer of 1971 he became more and more absorbed by the problems of the security situation. During these weeks the pressure from bomb and bullet increased and Northern Ireland's political institutions tottered under the strain. To those of us who tried to reach out to him he gave the assurance that he would do nothing rash – though he also stressed that, ultimately, security was his responsibility and his alone.

In August 1971 Faulkner decided that a 'Doomsday position was apparent'. At that point he reached for the most controversial of all his powers – internment. In a matter of weeks after offering the concept of a United Ulster he was now taking a course diametrically opposed to all he had been trying to say. Undoubtedly the pressures were great, but the miscalculation was massive in its implications. In resorting to internment

Faulkner had made his greatest mistake; he was now about to learn his greatest lesson; and learn he did.

REFERENCES AND NOTES

1   David Bleakley, *Faulkner* (Mowbray, 1974, p.79).
2   *Northern Ireland Hansard*, 22 June 1971.

PART FIVE

THE DISMANTLING OF STORMONT

CHAPTER 11

Internment – Turning Back the Clock

THE IRISH are no strangers to internment without trial – North and South the procedure has been used when the ruling parties have deemed the State to be in danger. Ministers, whatever their political persuasions, have been firm in their application of the system. Indeed, when it has been used by the Dublin government internment has often been accompanied by additional measures of the utmost severity.

But in the North – unlike in the South – the weapon has had a sectarian edge to it, making it unacceptable to the Catholic community. As a result, in the founding years of the Northern State, the Special Powers Act became one of the most controversial measures separating Protestant from Catholic. For the Catholic population internment was seen as a legal insult directed solely at Catholics; for them it became an intolerable example of the 'two people' tribal theory operating in the Province. Protestants, for the most part, though not particularly enthusiastic about the Special Powers Act, tended to regard it as a necessary evil, to be used to defend the Province against armed attacks on the lives and property of Northern Ireland citizens. During and after the Second World War, tensions eased in Northern Ireland; memories of earlier passions faded as the entire Province benefited from welfare state legislation. Important differences still remained, but a sense of community oneness began to emerge. Many who subscribed to the new view of things no longer saw themselves as belonging to neat 'Orange' or 'Green' categories – new blends were being tried. Indeed, no longer was it easy to identify religion by an attitude to the border issue. As independent surveys revealed, considerable numbers of Catholics and anti-Unionist Party Protestants favoured British citizenship. There was in fact, in the 1950s and 1960s, evidence of a considerable 'third' force in the Ulster community – the concept of a united Province was beginning to challenge the more traditional United Ireland or divided Ulster alternatives. Pluralism was on the way.

As one of Ireland's most far-seeing Church leaders, Cardinal Cahal Daly, has remarked about the outbreak of physical violence in the North: 'The tragedy is that the incipient growth of understanding and mutual acceptance which marked the ten years up to August 1969 has now been blighted by the frost of violence'. Many shared his view. For such reasons, when in the early 1960s the Special Powers Act fell into disuse, few people really mourned its departure; though still on the Statute Book, it had been effectively repealed by public opinion.

Faulkner was less certain of this repeal. During his period as Minister of Home Affairs he had inherited the internment policy of his predecessors and became convinced that the Special Powers Act was necessary for the security operations of his department. On becoming Prime Minister in 1971 his interest in security was undiminished. Responsibility was shared with no other minister and he made sure of his monopoly by combining the office of Prime Minister with that of Home Affairs. This was a considerable double burden to shoulder – he became involved in law and order situations which hampered the more embracing community role he needed to develop as leader of the Province. Politically he developed a split personality.

No doubt he recognized the need to use the powers of the Home Affairs Ministry with discretion; and it was also clear that Faulkner was anxious to use internment only as a last resort. He was pressed continually by many in Cabinet and Parliament to use his powers of detention, but he insisted on having sole personal responsibility in the matter and indicated that he would only move when there were 'clear security reasons' for doing so. A 'Doomsday situation', as he often told us, was what would persuade him to move. But what he never seemed to realize was that in such a sensitive area as internment there were implications which went well beyond purely security reasons. And, because he depended heavily on the military and civil service for advice, he was unlikely to be kept aware of those aspects which were important to Cabinet colleagues involved in the development of enterprises needing community cooperation. My own Department tried to redress the balance.

The military were particularly insistent on firm action. Sir Harry Tuzo, G.O.C. Northern Ireland, warned: 'I doubt if there is anybody now raising their voice at the possibility of internment who could really feel surprised or aggrieved if it were introduced after the chain of outrages which have occurred and which they appear to condone. Obviously if the kind of indiscriminate and utterly brutal action being perpetuated by the

IRA were to continue they should not be surprised if this type of measure has to be introduced to protect the communuty.'[1]

By the middle of 1971 Faulkner was convinced that his 'Doomsday situation' was appearing. For some months there had been a sharp escalation in violence and in July bomb attacks were taking place at the rate of three a day (in 1971 there were over a thousand explosions in the Province). Casualties were heavy (38 killed between January and August) and many hundreds were injured. In addition, confidential reports were warning of a danger to water and electricity supplies as bombing attacks became more coordinated. There were also reports of foreign-based organizations aiding terrorist groupings.

On top of the security situation there was a catastrophic political deterioration. In July the SDLP decided to withdraw from the Stormont Parliament and to set up a rival assembly of their own. This, coming after the warm reception to his June proposals for parliamentary participation, greatly disappointed Faulkner and he promptly accused them of giving in to the 'hard men of Republicanism' who, he claimed, had made it clear to the SDLP that they were expected not to play a part at Stormont – however constructive a part they were offered – but to tear it down. He genuinely mourned the passing of his political initiative of a few months earlier which now seemed light years away.

With the apparent failure of his plans for Stormont, Faulkner became more absorbed in security problems. The 'indiscriminate and brutal activities' castigated by Tuzo continued. In response, on 9 August 1971, the Prime Minister of Northern Ireland announced that internment had become necessary because 'no major alternative means of bringing the situation under control could be recommended by the security forces'. It was, as he put it, a 'very grave decision' taken 'in the light of the security advice and after consultation with Mr Heath and senior members of the United Kingdom Government'.

But it was also a very lonely decision and deliberately so. Faulkner trusted his own judgement on security matters and was reluctant to discuss details in any meaningful way with his cabinet colleagues. Rarely was the whole Cabinet given an opportunity to have a full-scale discussion on the subject. Security had indeed been the last item on the agenda at a July cabinet meeting before their leaving for the holidays, but even at this late stage there was no indication of a new move. Members were encouraged on their way and were given the usual instructions to be available should they be needed during the summer vacation. But nothing more was said as they dispersed for the traditional holiday period. The Prime Minister's parting advice to me was: 'Come back refreshed for the battle' – little did I know!

In the event the Minister of Community Relations, who must have a special concern with such a sensitive subject as internment, was not consulted. The first I knew of the decision to intern was in a BBC report heard while I was on a touring holiday in Cornwall – at, of all places, Lands End! I had been in daily telephone contact with my very able and alert Permanent Secretary, Bill Slinger, in Belfast, but no prior warning had been given. Such was the secrecy of the Prime Minister on security matters – his confidants were restricted to a personal circle, the military and civil service.

The internment operation when it did come in the early hours of 9 August 1971 was swift and spectacular. At 4.30 a.m. the army moved in on a provincewide operation. Within an hour 300 men had been removed from their homes to the specially prepared troop-ship Maidstone, which was to become a prison ship until Long Kesh camp was available. A few hours later the world heard Brian Faulkner's announcement:

> I have had to conclude that the ordinary law cannot deal comprehensively or quickly enough with such ruthless viciousness. I have therefore decided after weighing all the relevant considerations, including the views of the security forces and after consultations with Her Majesty's Government in the United Kingdom last Thursday, to exercise, where necessary, the powers of detention and internment vested in me as Minister of Home Affairs.

Meanwhile as the arrests went on Faulkner, locked away in solitude in Stormont Castle, signed Order after Order serving detention on those who, he had been assured, were the cause of all his security trouble. But within hours of signing hundreds of these documents it had become obvious that all was not going according to plan; it had all the marks of a botched operation. Many of those arrested were 'yesterday's men' – veterans from old records or newcomers whose names were culled from student and other protest movements. Some important IRA leaders were taken, but most had got away in good time. It was also clear that the IRA 'class of 1971' was composed of a new generation quite unknown to those on whom Faulkner had relied for advice.

For a while the Ministry of Home Affairs and the army claimed great things for the new initiative, but, in fact, far from causing violence to diminish, internment released a new flood of communal tension. As the first arrests began, street battles were taking place throughout the Province. Barricades were built and hundreds of homes were set alight as a 'scorched earth' policy gripped the 'peace line' areas. The house-burnings were flashed to every television station in the world. There followed a terrible communal migration which created 8,000 refugees in one week in Belfast and eventually uprooted 60,000 people, as each side, fearing the other, sought refuge in areas controlled by fellow Protestants or Catholics.

Internment may not have created these problems, but it added greatly to them and struck a mighty blow at the community organizations dedicated to a policy and programme of reconciliation. Roman Catholics everywhere were affronted.

Predictably, the Catholic community erupted with unbelief and anger when internment was announced. Faulkner tried hard to reassure them: 'I want to say a word to my Catholic fellow countrymen. I do not for one moment confuse your community with the IRA or imagine that these acts of terror have been committed in your name or with your approval. I have always had great respect for the God-fearing people – albeit with personal views different from my own – I have met in every part of Ulster.' He continued: 'We are now trying to remove the shadow of fear which hangs over too many of you. I appeal to you to come out and join us in building this community up again – not to restore it simply to what it was, for many of us in the past have failed each other, but to build it on better, sounder and stronger lines. Unless you take the place in the community which awaits you all of us will be the losers. My door is open to any of your leaders, political or religious, who want to discuss how we can now move forward.'

This 'open door' appeal was, no doubt, sincerely meant, but it was tragically naive. Clearly the Prime Minister was convinced that it was possible to make a distinction between security methods and general policy. He was soon to learn how wrong he was. The Roman Catholic community was completely alienated and erupted with a show of solidarity that shook Ulster to its foundations. On 9 August 1971 the Ulster crisis entered a new and critical phase as Roman Catholics welded together and began to formulate united demands which took on a new and far-reaching dimension; consent to rule was being withdrawn. Time had not stood still since 1921.

Faulkner was soon made aware of Catholic reaction – often from those who a few months earlier had been giving him warm support. The *Belfast Irish News* was brutally frank on the day following internment: 'To ask as he did yesterday for the cooperation of the Catholic community in political affairs, after issuing orders for the arrest and internment of his political opponents is insincerity of the rankest sort. It is the hypocrisy of Tartuffe. Yesterday was a day of awful tragedy.' For Faulkner it was a personal tragedy. His early years in government had made him suspect by his Catholic countrymen and he had tried hard to create a new image in recent years. Work in Commerce and his early months as Prime Minister had won him a good deal of cross-community respect. August 1971 changed all that. Catholic leaders, North and South, flailed him as few had been flailed before. There were calls on all sides for his removal from office. Mr Lynch on behalf of the Dublin Government even demanded the abolition of Stormont. The Catholic Church added its criticism, with Cardinal Conway declaring that 'internment without trial is a terrible power to give a political authority'. The Cardinal also stated his 'abhorrence of internment without trial' and was particularly concerned about its 'one-sided application'. The Pope broke a two-year silence on the Northern Ireland problem with an appeal for peace which included an implied criticism of security policy.

Others more remote from Rome added their criticism. Dr Paisley accused the Prime Minister of introducing internment not as a weapon for constitutional defence, 'but as a weapon of purely political expediency to bolster up his own tottering Premiership'. He was joined in this comment by the then leading Protestant theoretician, Desmond Boal, MP, who called internment 'a legal monstrosity which is not only ineffective but which also can work hardship and injustice and in a sense is as unattractive as the situation it is meant to remedy'.

Faulkner pointed to support for his policy from many quarters, though as time went on it became more muted. Local Protestant Church leaders made a joint statement of general support, balanced with the hope that the system would operate as humanely as possible. The leaders 'recognised the necessity for the introduction of internment' because of 'the continuing violence and bloodshed for which there can be no justification'.

From British politicians, too, there was cautious support, usually in terms regretting the measure and hoping that it would be terminated as soon as possible. The Press were equally cautious though, except for the Irish papers, basically sympathetic. The liberal *Belfast Telegraph* complained that political as well as security considerations were behind the move but, 'in the state of the country today, Mr Faulkner and his security chiefs had little alternative other than give it a trial'. For the *Daily Mail* the decision meant that the army would no longer have to fight 'with both hands tied behind their backs'. *The Times* gave the comment: 'The situation is one which justifies the use of emergency powers'.

But what the outside world thought of internment was of less importance than its effect on the local situation. Very soon the Northern Ireland Government was faced with a whole series of problems consequent on the new security policy for which increasingly they had no answer.

The chief Catholic counter-attack was organized by the elected representatives of the Social Democratic and Labour Party, the Nationalist Party and the Republican Labour Party. These groups organized a provincewide and world-supported campaign of civil disobedience in which Stormont suffered the fury and fate felt by Captain Boycott in a previous century of Irish protest. Faulkner was now exposed on every front.

The conference of representatives expressed 'total opposition to internment' which they regarded as further proof of 'the total failure of the system of Government in Northern Ireland'. A five-point plan amounting to a policy of non-cooperation was agreed:

1. We call upon all those who hold public positions in Northern Ireland, whether elected or appointed, to express their opposition to internment by an immediate withdrawal from their positions and to announce it publicly without delay to give evidence that the system of Government set up by the 1920 Act has failed.
2. We call on the general public to participate in this protest by immediately withholding all rents and rates. We expect 100 per cent support from all opponents of internment and all opponents of the Ulster regime.
3. We will give our full support to all organisations who call meetings to oppose internment and appeal for complete unity in every area.
4. We demand that the military resume the task for which they were sent here – the protection of people and areas against sectarian attack on their homes, pending a political solution.
5. We call on the Westminster Government to suspend immediately the system of Government in Northern Ireland in view of its absolute failure to provide peace and stability in Northern Ireland and to institute immediate talks on new political and constitutional arrangements.[2]

The meeting also arranged to send representatives to Westminster and Dublin to express their views. So the Catholic community was welded together in a community reaction which could only lead to further confrontation – Northern Ireland was approaching the brink.

A few on either side saw the danger of a total community split and tried desperately to keep lines of communication open. They saw that certain forms of civil disobedience were very difficult to reverse and they also feared that rent and rate strikes by one community could just as easily be practised by another.

Typical of a few spokesmen from the Catholic community who warned against the dangers inherent in such a civil disobedience campaign was the comment of Dr G. B. Newe, secretary of the Northern Ireland Council of Social Service: 'Withdrawal from community structures means that true dialogue becomes impossible. One cannot have dialogue with an absent man! And where honest dialogue is inhibited or impossible, a breeding ground for suspicion and mistrust is created. Bombing turns people off; so does a rhetoric of exclusion. We desperately need a great dose of social charity without which it will be impossible to achieve social justice.'[3]

Faulkner responded to the civil disobedience threat by ordering every department to indicate the extent to which civil disobedience would affect its operations. In Cabinet we saw at once that there was no agreed response open to the government. Uniquely and dangerously, the civil service had no guide lines on which to operate. It was also impossible to treat civil disobedience with a cessation of services. A whole population could not be cut off from essential supplies. Equally, entire estates could not be evicted for rent arrears; nor could electricity supplies be terminated when there were those who would immediately reconnect. The possibility of a slide into anarchy was sensed in the 'corridors of power'.

The Northern Ireland Government soon discovered how much civilization depends on the consent and cooperation of those who comprise society. Consent had been withdrawn from the system; it would only be restored when security policies (and as time went on, much else) were reversed. Internment had indeed become a Pandora's box.

Faulkner had now reached his ultimate confrontation; and his advice to his colleagues was to 'just grit our teeth and try to pursue a commonsense line which will have both security and political aspects'. Cabinet meetings became increasingly solemn.

When the Northern Ireland Parliament resumed in October after the summer recess Faulkner was still putting a brave face on things and in a defiant speech made a vigorous appeal which was Churchillian in its tone. Speaking to those 'who are working to destroy Ulster', he had this to say:

> 'We shall resist you. We shall resist you as a Parliament; we shall resist you as a people. To protect our way of life we will make any sacrifice and endure any hardship. We have had divisions which have given comfort to our enemies; we can, and I believe we must, put such divisions behind us. You have destroyed our property, bullied our people and made many live in fear. All of these things only increase our resolve to resist you. You cannot win for we shall not permit it.'

But Churchill would have been addressing such words to a foreign power; Faulkner was castigating fellow citizens.

About such sentiments there was a blinding sense of unreality. There was now no 'Parliament' of Northern Ireland – there were two (Stormont and an Assembly of the Northern Ireland People); nor was there a 'people' – tragically, there was a reversion to Catholic and Protestant. Internment, aimed at hindering the men of violence, had become the cause of even greater suffering to the whole community. I had often reminded Faulkner of the *sui generis* nature of community relations – the phrase used by House of Commons Speaker Selwyn Lloyd to describe my unusual appointment to the post – but we still had some way to go before we fully agreed on the centrality of community relations to good government.

The essential difference was brought out in an exchange of letters between Faulkner and his Minister of Community Relations, following my departure from the Government in September 1971. In my letter of resignation I stated my objection to internment in sentiments which reflected the concern of supporters of the Labour movement and, indeed, a wider spectrum of public opinion: 'I cannot accept that the policy of internment is assisting the cause of law and order. On the contrary I believe that internment is wrong; that this aspect of our policy is a tragic mistake which has made matters worse; further I believe that the terrorists welcome internment for it gives the IRA and other militant groups a sympathy and a hearing on a worldwide scale which otherwise they could not get. In addition, the internment controversy handicaps those who are presenting the Northern Ireland case against the campaign of violence.'

The letter also dealt with the community-divisive elements of internment – an aspect which cut right across the united Ulster theme which in his June speech Faulkner had been highlighting with signal success.

'Internment is not, as some see it, an isolated security issue; it is a test of policy direction. More than any single issue, it separates Protestant and Roman Catholic and tragically it has alienated the Roman Catholic community at the very moment when community cooperation is most vital.' Finally I stressed the united Ulster point: 'In fact, in the Ulster of today we just cannot have internment and a united community. And without a united community a really worthwhile Province is impossible. Those who think otherwise betray a dangerous degree of political insensitivity.'[4]

For me internment day 1971 became yet another defining moment in my personal journey through Irish politics. I felt something of the dismay and shock experienced by my Catholic fellow citizens. Like the leading businessman who telephoned me in desperation: 'What am I to say to my student sons who bitterly insist that this proves that the IRA are right after all?' I shared his desperation; I was ashamed at what my government had done to fellow citizens such as these; I feared for the future of my Province, which needed Protestant and Catholic unity as never before.

By New Year 1972 few believed that Faulkner had long to go. However, he had no intention of resigning and knew that he had no serious rival in Stormont. What he did not realize was that Edward Heath was preparing more far-reaching plans of his own: Direct Rule from Westminster. Already in the closing months of 1971 many hints were given by Whitehall that a fundamental reassessment was being considered. Even Cabinet ministers in Belfast began to sense that both Heath and Maudling were toying with new ideas. Only Brian Faulkner seemed unaware that plans for a take-over were well advanced. Fatally, he had begun to believe his own propaganda.

REFERENCES AND NOTES

1   Personal papers, David Bleakley.
2   Bleakley, *Faulkner* (Mowbray, 1974, p.101) (SDLP).
3   Bleakley, *Faulkner* (Mowbray, 1974, p.102).
4   Bleakley, Diary, September 1971.

CHAPTER 12

Direct Rule – Almost a Colony

IN FAULKNER'S LIFETIME Irish 'Faulkneralia' was splendidly extravagant – cutting, yet at the same time containing a tang of admiration. Like the one commenting on the famous capacity to survive, whatever the hazard: *Question* – 'If Faulkner fell under a bus tomorrow, what on earth would happen?' *Answer* – 'The bloody bus would miss him!' So it was with the calamity of internment – Faulkner survived.

Matters came to a climax early in 1972. It was clear that the security operation was not going well – military sources were pressing hard for a complete transfer of security powers to London. The demands became even more urgent after the shooting in Londonderry, by the army, of thirteen civilians during a demonstration in January. These tragic killings, which passed into history as 'Bloody Sunday', made a dramatic impression on London thinking and probably more than any other single incident sealed the Direct Rule decision. When the end came it came suddenly. Faulkner was invited to meet Heath and his colleagues in Downing Street. There, at a meeting on 22 March 1972, the Prime Minister put it to him bluntly: the United Kingdom Government had decided to take over complete control of security matters, including all matters to do with the courts in Northern Ireland; the Stormont Government could continue in office, but with much reduced local powers. Faulkner was not impressed and was equally blunt in reaction.

But the 'bloody bus' had missed Ulster's demoted Prime Minister once again. By an ironic quirk of fate Edward Heath's historic intervention gave Faulkner an opportunity to survive and to revive his fortunes. No longer was he bedevilled by internment and the other security problems which had diverted him from more positive programmes. From now on the odium and difficulty of security matters passed to the British Government and the address for future complaints would be Whitehall. Faulkner was now freed to be his 'own man' and to enter into the debate about the formation of the new Ulster which he sensed to be at hand. It was to be a vital debate.

'Direct Rule', as the Westminster take-over of the Stormont administration in March 1972 was called, was a traumatic experience for the people of Northern Ireland. Many feared the development; others saw it as a necessary step in the creation of a new and better Province; but there were few who welcomed the event without reservations.

Most Ulster people, however, recognized the decision of the British Government to rule the Province directly from London as a watershed, ending the political arrangement imposed by the Government of Ireland Act, 1920. Mr Heath's intervention had destroyed the power monopoly enjoyed by the Unionist Party. From then on it was regarded as inevitable that the creation of any new framework for government would have to take into account the religious balance of the population and the tensions associated with the crisis before and since 1969. No doubt the planners in Whitehall had some such plan in mind when they advised the move in March 1972; equally clearly, they were less aware of the nature of the difficulties which lay ahead, or of the grave new options which would confront them as confidence between Belfast and London eroded.

For Brian Faulkner the actual moment of Direct Rule was bitter. He had trusted Edward Heath and had been confident that the trust was reciprocated. The two men had known each other throughout their political careers and shared much in common. They had been Whips together, each had been in Board of Trade departments at the same time, and each had gained the top office in government. Socially they came from similar backgrounds and had fought a lone battle to the summit. Even their personalities were related – both were strong-willed, not all that at ease on the gregarious occasion, and enjoyed the more solitary pastime of sailing. But between them there could be no real parity of esteem. Each was, no doubt, determined to have his own way, but in such a confrontation Heath had the advantage: Section 75 of the Government of Ireland Act gave Westminster the final authority in Northern Ireland affairs. Heath was also anxious that nothing should happen in Northern Ireland to interfere with his European policy. Already, embarrassing questions had been raised by EEC colleagues and, on security in particular, the Ulster situation had involved the United Kingdom Government internationally in a difficult defence of the policy – for example, by derogation from the European Human Rights Convention.

Faulkner recognized these difficulties, but was still confident of the Prime Minister's support. He had been assured by his frequent visits to Downing Street that all was well – indeed, Faulkner believed firmly that he had established a special relationship with the British Premier which would preserve the constitutional status quo.

For these reasons Faulkner felt a sense of personal affront when he received Heath's ultimatum on 22 March 1972. He had come to the meeting at Downing Street believing that agreed new initiatives would be discussed. As he stated later, he had gone fully prepared to acknowledge that in defeating the violence, military measures would have to be buttressed by political proposals, designed to unite the communities. The Northern Ireland Government had already submitted a comprehensive letter of proposals in preparation for such a discussion. But instead of the expected conference, Faulkner found himself faced not with a wider-ranging review of such reforms, but with a proposition which he held to be wholly unacceptable – that all statutory and executive responsibility for law and order should be vested in the United Kingdom Parliament and Government. This included criminal law and procedure (including the organization of and appointments to the courts); public order; prisons and penal establishments; the determination of new penal offences; special powers; the public prosecuting power; and the police. And, as Faulkner stated later: 'Even these radical changes were simply to pave the way for further entirely open-ended discussions with continuing speculation and uncertainty.' Altogether it was very advanced political surgery. It was an operation unacceptable to Faulkner and his Cabinet. He had encountered a Premier as devious as himself!

Faulkner did not hesitate. He had already stated on many previous occasions (and this Heath knew) that his Government would not operate under such conditions which he regarded as 'an acceptance of totally baseless criticism of stewardship'. He indicated immediately that he was not interested in maintaining a Stormont that would be 'a mere sham, or a face-saving charade'. His resignation and that of his Cabinet followed, delayed only by the few days requested by Heath to ensure that there should be no breach in the orderly government of the country until the necessary transfer legislation passed through Westminster.

On his return to Belfast, Faulkner issued a last message to the people of Northern Ireland. He was sad and serious, but determined. After outlining the events leading to the final decision, he warned the British Government that many people would draw 'a sinister and depressing message from these events – that violence can pay; that violence does pay; that those who shout, lie, denigrate and even destroy can earn for themselves an attention that responsible conduct and honourable behaviour do not'.[1] He was angry but, as always, his anger was controlled. He warned about the danger of making matters worse through irresponsible reaction: 'I ask our people at this difficult and trying time to remain calm and on no account to be led by unwise agitation into possible confrontation with the security forces, which have been making such tremendous sacrifices on our behalf.' Then his final pledge: 'We will work, with total determination and utter firmness, but responsibly and under the law, to ensure that the voice of the Ulster majority – which is not a sectarian majority but a majority of responsible people loyal to the Crown – is heard loud and clear throughout the land.' (I noted at the time his new gloss on 'majority' – an indication of things to come.)

But Faulkner's initial anger was considerable and for a while he retaliated by lunging out at Heath at political meetings in Northern Ireland and Britain (and later in the USA). He rarely indulged in a counter-attack which was personal, but when he decided to do so he could be biting in retort. He made many comparisons with various forms of dictatorship and accused Heath of betraying the Province and of trying to set up a 'coconut colony'; he also warned that the British Government were releasing forces which they did not understand and might not be able to control. Such sentiments made a considerable impression on the Ulster public and he began to win back some of the support which had been lost in the period following internment. (When some months later the *Belfast Telegraph* carried out a leadership support poll, 44 per cent of the Protestant vote went to Faulkner, with Craig and Paisley getting 15 per cent and 13 per cent respectively.) Heath, too, noted these attacks, and from then on relationships between the two leaders cooled rapidly. When they met later at the 1973 Sunningdale Conference it was obvious to the other participants that the 'special relationship' had become one of wary coolness. Some regarded it as distinctly icy. As one observer later recalled: 'Heath was determined to drive Faulkner into the ground.' In fact, the Irish, North and South, showed signs of sympathy for Faulkner – a useful bonus.

Significantly, Faulkner was not alone in regretting the passing of Stormont. He got the support of constituency organizations throughout the country and even his right-wing critic, Vanguard leader William Craig, felt able to say: 'Our Prime Minister did his best and he was shabbily treated.' More surprising, influential voices in the Roman Catholic community expressed regrets. From G. B. Newe, his Catholic colleague in the Cabinet, came a comment which gave expression to the sense of something Irish having been lost: 'As an Irishman I am sorry that an Irish Parliament has been disbanded. Of course, I would have preferred Northern Ireland to be governed by Irishmen rather than by Englishmen. I hope that sooner or later an Irish administration will return to Northern Ireland.'[1]

Eddie McAteer, the leader of the Nationalist Party, was equally conscious of the Irish dimension: 'This is a day of sadness for I find no joy in being ruled from the remote and insensitive smoke-rooms of Westminster. Faced with the choice I would prefer to be ruled by Protestant Irishmen than by Englishmen.' And then, a percipient hint at things to come: 'Perhaps we will now at last find common ground as equal people without sectarian power, perhaps as brothers 'agin' the Government. A terrible beauty has not quite been born, but the pregnancy is well advanced.'[2] In both communities there were many who shared McAteer's reaction.

One hundred and seventy-two years earlier something of the same sense of loss had been felt in Ireland when the Act of Union closed another Irish Parliament. 'A poor thing but our own', was the view of many in Ulster about Stormont.

Faulkner, never given to the long-term forecasts, preferred to get on with the task in hand. As his initial anger passed, he began to look for ways to regain the initiative and to make sure that he retained his grasp on the leadership of the country. The power vacuum was worrying so he decided to fill it as quickly as possible. By leading the local criticism against Westminster he had already managed to behave like a Prime Minister-in-waiting, and with his assured wealth he had no difficulty in continuing the lifestyle associated with the office. He also had support behind the scenes from top civil servants who, though they were loyal to the incoming administration, felt and hoped that one day local ministers would return.

But Faulkner also realized the realities of Westminster power and the need to re-establish himself at home and abroad. In a spectacular tour of England and Scotland (followed later by a coast-to-coast visit to America) he began his national and international comeback, presenting his case as 'a loyal subject who had done his best' and who had been sacrificed by the appeasement policy of a British Prime Minister who had 'a very poor opinion indeed of the British public's moral fibre'. This was popular material among the Tory rank-and-file and very rapidly regained him a firm following in the Conservative Party. Even the Bow Group were impressed and provided an influential London platform at the Royal Commonwealth Society rooms at which he spelt out the ways in which he regarded Heath's initiative as 'morally and politically wrong'. He very astutely developed the theme that London intellectuals had taken over from the down-to-earth politicians in Belfast (though, some of his listeners must have murmured, 'Indeed, they have and near time, too'!): 'For Mr Heath and Mr Wilson and Mr Thorpe the affairs of Northern Ireland are a matter of political science . . . for us in Ulster it is a matter of life and death.' The Tory Party was increasingly impressed by this point of view and a few months later, when Faulkner addressed the Conservative annual conference, he was given a rapturous welcome. Neither Edward Heath nor William Whitelaw seemed to enjoy the occasion but, no doubt, they took the point.

While consolidating his support in Britain, Faulkner at the same time turned to the problem of reorganizing his Unionist home base. Since 1969 dangerous schisms had appeared and he felt the need to build a united front. Two ideas in particular, as alternatives to Direct Rule, were challenging the former monolithic unity of the Unionist Party – various forms of independence and total integration with Britain. The Unionist pressure group Vanguard, with the support of one of Faulkner's chief rivals, former Cabinet Minister William Craig, openly discussed new forms of constitutional relationships between Belfast and London. The long-term aims of the Vanguard Movement worried Faulkner. He noted that Craig for some time had been talking about a fundamentally new relationship between Ulster and Britain, in which Ulster would achieve – ideally by negotiation – an independent status, with appropriate links with the Crown and the Commonwealth. In view of the impossibility of getting local and national consent for such an aim, many people regarded such a policy as, in essence, a UDI demand.

Faulkner believed that programmes based on a thesis of independence were 'absolute rubbish'; there was therefore an unbridgeable gulf between him and the Vanguard leader. The nature of the divide became apparent during 1972 as Faulkner and Craig both made their proposals. For Faulkner the challenge was one of working within the options offered by Direct Rule and the constitutional guarantees offered by Westminster, while at the same time working towards the re-establishment of a local parliament. Vanguard, for its part, looked for a fresh Constitution which would allow for 'a new model of political relationships in the British Isles in which Great Britain, Ulster and Eire would be independent entities with, hopefully, better relationships between them'. Also at another Vanguard rally it was resolved to work for the restoration of the Northern Ireland Parliament 'preferably within the United Kingdom, but if necessary without'.

It was the suggestion of a Northern Ireland Parliament 'without' the United Kingdom that caused Faulkner to swerve most swiftly from the Vanguard organization and which undoubtedly convinced him that no accommodation could be made with its supporters. For some months he persevered with Craig, trying to involve him in joint Unionist approaches to the British Government, but increasingly he felt it impossible to establish points of contact. Very soon he was hurling the 'UDI' accusation directly at the Movement – in so doing he won back much of the support lost during the internment debate. It was a vital exercise. By 'nipping in the bud' Craig's independence notions, Faulkner was keeping alive the possibility of Protestant–Catholic reconciliation.

Equal difficulties lay in the way of an agreement with Ian Paisley. The Democratic Unionist Party leader was quite clear in his denunciation of UDI and had prepared a very different response to Direct Rule – total integration with Britain. This demand was described by many as a 'gimmick' and, except for Enoch Powell, it found little favour among political leaders in Britain or Ireland. Emotionally, however, it had greater appeal than UDI and even Faulkner in his speech to the Bow Group saw merit in it. If something better than a 'sham Stormont' were not available then he would settle for nothing less than a full alignment with the rest of the United Kingdom on the Scottish pattern, giving adequate representation at Westminster, full British standards and a total equality with fellow citizens in Great Britain.

However, always a realist, Faulkner soon saw in subsequent meetings with British Ministers that integration was impossible – and the Labour Opposition were equally adamant. He also recognized that to press for such a policy as the only acceptable Ulster safeguard was to draw Belfast and London into a constitutionally dangerous process. In these circumstances, he believed that the best way to safeguard the Province as an integral part of the United Kingdom was through the re-establishment of an effective local parliament. For these reasons he believed that talk about total integration was counter-productive and diverted Ulster people away from the essential task which was to ensure that the new constitutional settlement which must come was in the best interests of Northern Ireland. So, as with William Craig, with Ian Paisley no accommodation was possible.

Faulkner's attempts in the early weeks of Direct Rule to probe the varied ranks of Unionism disturbed many local observers and many accused him of prevarication. But there were also those who saw evidence that he was feeling out the ground around him and testing opinion among the 'grass roots'; and his speeches on such mass-meeting occasions also ensured that mainstream Unionist opinion was heard. In any case, having made his reconnoitre, in typical fashion he decided to retire to reassess the situation.

Around this time, Brian Walker (later Director of Oxfam, but then leader of the New Ulster Movement) called on the local political leaders to lower their voices. In particular, he advised Faulkner to take a very long holiday and 'reassess the entirely new situation given to both communities by the Westminster initiatives'. It was good advice and Faulkner took it. In April 1972, after the most intense political period of his life, he set off along with his wife on a lengthy tour of France, Switzerland and Italy. It was a restful and reflective time – though on one occasion he was seen wandering in the Memorial Gardens in Geneva regarding the famous Martyrs, and no doubt wondering what was in store for him! In the weeks away from Ulster Faulkner made a fundamental reassessment which was to alter radically his own future and that of the community he aspired to lead: he began to realize with compelling clarity that a new Ulster could only be assembled within the framework of a new dynamic. And the dynamic was – partnership.

When Faulkner returned to Belfast his mind was made up: in private and public conversations he made it clear that a new accommodation must be sought with Westminster, within the context of the United Kingdom and in accordance with the concept of 'an active, permanent and guaranteed role' for both communities in Northern Ireland. It is an idea which has stood the test of time and which had been demanding attention since the inception of the State of Northern Ireland.

Ideas like these meant setting aside the political habits of a lifetime. Also revolutionary, for a Unionist leader, was acceptance of the notion that consent was an imperative for all in Ulster. And real consent demanded a two-way process, Protestant *and* Catholic. The unthinkable had at last become thinkable. There was only one way forward: Protestants and Catholics together in a shared community government. Brian Faulkner was about to embark on the final and greatest initiative of his political career.

REFERENCES AND NOTES

1 Bleakley, *Faulkner* (Mowbray, 1974, p.111).
2 *Ibid.*, p.111.

CHAPTER 13

Power Sharing, January–May 1974 – A Brief Encounter

'The British Government have a clear objective in Northern Ireland. It is to deliver its people from the violence and fear in which they live today and to set them free to realise their great potential to the full.'

WITH THOSE WORDS in 1972 William Whitelaw, Secretary of State for Northern Ireland, introduced his famous White Paper, 'The Future of Northern Ireland'. A few months later the Northern Ireland Constitution Act 1973 provided the Province with a new Constitution and Assembly. Thereafter followed one of the most tantalizing 'ifs' in Anglo-Irish history – 'if only the new Executive had been given more time' was the view of most observers.

But time the power-sharing Government did not get. After only five months, one of the most promising constitutional initiatives in the history of the Province, and of Ireland, was ended in the chaos caused by a politically-motivated General Strike. However, though short in duration, Brian Faulkner's power-sharing Government broke new ground in community politics – indeed, its sensible innovations in voting systems, devolution of power and models of inter-governmental cooperation offer models for improvement in other areas of Britain and Ireland which suffer from a democratic deficit. In any schemes of regional government in Scotland or Wales, the Ulster models would repay study.

In 1972 Northern Ireland was fortunate in its British Prime Minister (Edward Heath) and its Secretary of State (William Whitelaw), who each appreciated the gravity of what was proposed. Heath, for example, when

announcing on 24 March 1972 the suspension of the Stormont Government for one year, made clear to the Commons that the transfer was 'an
indispensable condition for progress in finding a political solution in
Northern Ireland'. With his usual firmness of purpose he mapped out an
agenda for action and provided the political and administrative back-up.
Many of us were surprised at his grasp of matters and his personal
commitment. Later on I began to appreciate more fully the preparedness
and concern which went into Edward Heath's thinking on Anglo-Irish
affairs.

In March 1982, I gave the Fellowship of Reconciliation Alex Wood
Memorial Lecture in Liverpool, on what was then a relatively novel theme
– 'A New Comity of Anglo-Celtic Peoples'. Mr Heath read the lecture and
in a friendly follow-up letter to me did a bit of fine tuning on my script –
just to keep the record straight! But the major thrust of his interesting
and informative letter had to do with the wider significance of the Sunningdale Agreement and raised issues which are as relevant now as they
were in 1973. I quote the letter in full and trust that the lessons it offers
will be noted by those entrusted to draw up a new agreement for Northern Ireland.

FROM: The Rt Hon. Edward Heath, M.B.E., M.P.

House of Commons
7 September 1982

Dear Mr Bleakley,

I have spent part of the Parliamentary recess reading your
Alex Wood Memorial Lecture on 'Ireland and Britain
1660–1990 – a search for peace'.

I did so with interest, in particular the guidelines for a solution on pages 10 and 11, the suggestions for making 'interim
direct rule' more effective on pages 12 and 14 and your theme
of an interdependent British Isles on pages 19–21.

As you will no doubt be making further contributions on this
subject – at least I hope you will – perhaps I may make the
following comments for your consideration on future
occasions.

On page 15 you mention the emergence now of 'a triangular
pattern' between London, Belfast and Dublin. In fact this is
not new. I brought together the three Prime Ministers of the
United Kingdom, Northern Ireland and the Irish Republic for
the first time for nearly fifty years at Chequers in order to
discuss precisely this. It was the prelude to the Sunningdale
Agreement between the North, South and U.K. Governments
of 1973.

Which brings me to my next point.

I am somewhat surprised to say the least that with the exception of a mention in two separate half sentences on pages 11
and 13 you pay no attention whatever to the Sunningdale
Agreement and the power-sharing executive which followed it.
The Sunningdale Agreement was the first and, so far, the only
agreement voluntarily signed by the three component entities
of which you write. It was brought about by the long and
patient negotiation for which you plead. The Executive worked
efficiently and well in the interests of Northern Ireland until
the subsequent U.K. Labour Government under Mr Wilson
failed to give it the support it required from H.M. Forces to
break the petrol lorry drivers strike in May 1974.

The lesson to be learnt from that episode is that without
such support, either from its own resources or from the
United Kingdom Government, no administration in Northern
Ireland will ever survive.

Moreover, the Sunningdale Agreement was freely accepted
by Dublin as the basis for all future relations with the North as
well as with the United Kingdom. We have now dropped a
long way back from that position. Relationships appear never
to have been worse. [A judgement also made in Garret Fitzgerald's autobiography.]

As far as your concluding theme [Interdependent British
Isles] is concerned this would have been much more likely of
fulfilment if the policy of devolution developed over the ten
years of my leadership of the British Conservative Party had
been implemented by my successors. Alas, it has been repu-
diated by the present leadership. You will find the task of rec-
reating support for such a constitutional development in
Britain just as difficult as your task of reconciliation in Northern Ireland.

Perhaps I may be permitted one personal comment. It is not
true to say, page 2, that I 'have had little real contact with the
island'. From the late fifties onwards I stayed privately with
friends in Northern Ireland where I was able to see for myself
the conditions there and discuss the problems with people of
varying views. In the early sixties I also visited Northern Ireland officially in connection with Britain's first negotiations to
become a member of the European Economic Community. I
then met not only members of the Government and officials
but also those connected with business and the Trade Unions. I
continued my visits after I became leader of the British Conservative Party in 1965. In addition, leaders of the Opposition
in Stormont discussed their problems with me at my home in
London. You may well be right that no Englishman can fully

understand Irish affairs but at least those of us who try to remedy our limitations might be given some little credit for so doing. My one regret is that having positions in Government at Westminster for so many years since 1951 I have never been able to gain an equivalent knowledge and personal experience of the Republic of Ireland.

I wish you well in your endeavours.

Yours sincerely,

Edward Heath

Northern Ireland was well served by Prime Minister Heath; it was a pity that soon after the appointment of a power-sharing Government both he and his Secretary of State departed at a critical point in the evolution of the new Executive. Labour Premier Harold Wilson never carried the authority or cautious trust given to Edward Heath. Indeed, Wilson was regarded as something of a covert republican; a 'persuader', long before the Labour Party in 1981 (and endorsed in 1994) adopted the constitutionally bizarre policy of committing itself to the aim of a united Ireland by consent, along with the equally divisive notion of a 'persuader' role for future Labour Governments. By promoting such an approach to Irish affairs, Harold Wilson cut the British Labour Party off from the great majority of Ulster trade unionists and from many socialists in the North who had borne the heat of the day in service to their sister Party. Heath, more attuned to the realities of Irish life, saw the historic and effective role of a British Government as being one of a facilitator for reconciliation. He talked of 'a chance for fairness, a chance for prosperity, a chance for peace, a chance at last to bring the bombings and killings to an end' (Commons, 24 March 1972). Such language got to the heart of the matter.

The Secretary of State who was presented with this agenda was well chosen. William Whitelaw was something new in Irish politics – an Englishman whom everyone trusted. Even when deemed wrong he was forgiven with a friendly 'He means well, anyway' comment. This avuncular and shrewd Tory giant was the right man in the right place at the right time. In a land of superlative talkers he talked everyone into a kind of sanity and made possible combinations which not many politicians in Ireland or elsewhere had previously attempted. Few English statesmen have left such a decisive mark on Ireland in such a short time; when he left in 1973 there was great regret and apprehension at his departure. The apprehension was well founded.

Early days in the newly elected Northern Ireland Assembly (first meeting July 1973) were promising, if somewhat boisterous. The composition of the 78-member body, elected by proportional representation, brought together a membership cross-community in composition and considerable in talent. New voices were present representing a more broadly based nationalism, within the Social Democratic and Labour Party (SDLP), and providing a blend of rural nationalism and Catholic working-class radicals from Belfast and Derry. Socialist republican Gerry Fitt led the group which was rich in talent. So, too, was the recently formed interdenominational Alliance Party of Northern Ireland (APNI), bringing together Protestants and Catholics with the primary purpose of a political crusade against sectarian politics.

All this was good for Ulster politics. Unfortunately it was particularly destructive of the trade union-based Northern Ireland Labour Party, whose candidates suffered the predictable fate of falling between the new stools of SDLP and Alliance. Each of these new groups, untrammelled by links with British Labour and the trade unions, were able to siphon off much of the NILP's long-standing and considerable traditional vote. As the liberal *Belfast Telegraph* said at the time in a sympathetic gesture to Labour candidates: 'There is not real room for more than one non-sectarian party in Northern Ireland.' It is to be hoped that this judgement will not stand the test of time. My hope and that of succeeding generations must be that eventually *all* parties in Northern Ireland will be non-sectarian in composition and political aspiration.

However, for official Labour (NILP) there was no new dawn in 1973. My colleagues were decimated at the polls and I became the sole NILP member in the new Assembly. There were some consolation compliments. For example, I was approached to accept the Presidency of the Assembly, an honour which I felt unable to accept in view of my party obligations. However, members in general and Secretary of State Whitelaw, and later Merlyn Rees, accorded me rights through all the 'usual channels'. In fact, as a 'member without Whip' I was often used in honest-broker undertakings and was certainly able to observe the Assembly scene without hindrance. There was much in the way of unparliamentary behaviour which was intolerable (Faulkner was interrupted one hundred and four times during his Sunningdale Conference report speech); but the essential core work of the Assembly was constructive and considerable; at its best Stormont could always hold its own with sister parliaments elsewhere.

The NI Assembly could have 'made it', if wider events had not intervened. For example, a first ever system of cross-party collective responsibility was established and worked well until the final stages of the Assembly. Individual ministers, regardless of religion or party, won public approval. Austin Currie of SDLP, for instance, took on the difficult problem of rent strikes and house allocation, with courage and success; Paddy Devlin was unanimously regarded as an outstanding defender of the Health Service and the rights of marginalized groups; his SDLP colleague John Hume won praise for his success overseas in attracting new employers and new jobs. Alliance's Oliver Napier, as Legal Minister, brought an increased confidence in the courts system, while Unionists like

Basil McIvor pushed ahead on the educational front. Prime Minister Faulkner could have no complaints about the efficiency of his Executive members.

In all this work a key role was played by Faulkner's deputy, Gerard (Gerry) Fitt, M.P., noted at Westminster as M.P. for West Belfast and now as a popular House of Lord's member. Gerry Fitt, one of the most amiable and colourful men in Irish politics, was born in Belfast in 1926 and had lived and worked for most of his life in the dockland area of the city. Leader of the nineteen-strong Social Democratic and Labour Party in the Northern Ireland Assembly, he had been associated with trade union and Labour politics from his boyhood days. Though as Irish and nationalist as any of his colleagues, Fitt's Belfast connection had brought him into contact with a political cross-section of the Province, an advantage which those who came from the remoter and rural areas of the North did not have; it enabled him to bring to Catholic radicalism a deeper appreciation of the totality of Ulster life than any other nationalist leader. He was emphatically an Ulsterman and, as he put it, had 'more in common with a Belfast Protestant than a Catholic from Cork'.

But above all else, Fitt was a realist. Like Faulkner, by 1972 he had come to terms with the facts of local life and had realized the need to practise survival politics; he had no time for 'long-distance republicans' commenting far from the action. Fitt's influence was evident in the programme of his party in the Assembly election and was crucial in moving SDLP members towards accepting the principle of local consent. This local emphasis was far removed from the traditional nationalist stress on 'the whole Irish nation' and made possible a fundamental realignment in Northern politics which contributed substantially to the partnership formula. Fitt appreciated Faulkner's contribution to that formula and signalled his gratitude in the Assembly: 'I personally believe that Brian Faulkner has shown remarkable courage in trying to drag the Unionist Party into the twentieth century.'

Even the public often thought of them as a pair. Neither was regarded as one who stuck rigidly to points of dogma and each had a popular reputation of being something of a 'fixer'. They were known as men who believed in getting things done, and though they were sometimes accused of dealing an occasional card from the bottom of the political pack, they were widely regarded as people who would keep the game going. Such was the local folk-lore about these two party stalwarts who, in the summer of 1973, began to move towards a union without precedent in Ulster politics.

Oddly enough, when the partnership was announced it received rapid and widespread acceptance. A few years earlier, such a combination would have seemed impossible; by 1973 there was a touch of inevitability about it, encouraging widespread acceptance.

But of more importance, the coming together of Faulkner and Fitt was a symbolic gesture between two people which made possible the greater partnership between the two traditions in Northern Ireland. From then onwards the point was increasingly made: 'If lifelong opponents like Gerry Fitt and Brian Faulkner get together, why not the rest of us?'

But before the Executive 'designate' could become an Executive 'appointed', there was one further stage – one which later was to involve Faulkner in fatal conflict with many of his supporters – the Sunningdale Conference convened by the British Government at Sunningdale, Berkshire, in December. The British Government had indicated in its White Paper of March 1973 that, following elections to the Assembly, it would invite the government of the Republic of Ireland and the leaders of the elected representatives of Northern Ireland opinion to participate with them in a conference to discuss how the three objectives set out in the Paper for discussion might best be pursued. These objectives were:

a) the acceptance of the present status of Northern Ireland, and the possibility – which would have to be compatible with the principle of consent – of subsequent change in that status;
b) effective consultation and cooperation in Ireland for the benefit of North and South alike; and
c) the provision of a firm basis for concerted governmental and community action against terrorist organisations.

The SDLP members of the Executive-designate were interested, in particular, in the 'Irish dimension' element in the proposed agenda; Faulkner Unionists were anxious to get effective joint action on security matters; and for all concerned there was a good deal of unspoken agreement that a successful conference was part of the price that had to be paid to enable the new Northern Ireland Executive to operate with success. The SDLP were particularly interested in this last point.

Faulkner had no doubts about the decision to go to Sunningdale. He felt that the Province had managed to regain much: a regional government was re-established with considerable powers and with growth potential; the border referendum had been decisively pro-Union; and the British Government had given firm guarantees about the future constitutional status of the Province. He was once again to be Chief Minister in Northern Ireland and had become the first leader of that state to speak for a significant proportion of both Protestant and Catholic communities. In addition, he had gained a considerable personal victory at the June general election and his group was still the largest in the Assembly. He felt in control of events once again and believed he could 'sell' the outcome of Sunningdale to his followers at home.

Subsequent events indicated that he was over-confident. In particular, his acceptance of a Council of Ireland was declared by his opponents as a sell-out, giving the Dublin Government an opportunity to share control with the U.K. Government in the governing of Northern Ireland. A misleading but damaging slogan was raised: 'An Irish Republic is only a Sunningdale Away'. When tested at the polls a few months later pro-Faulkner candidates were swept away in an avalanche of constitutional fear.

Yet from a calm reading of the agreed communiqué issued at the end of the Sunningdale Conference, it is clear that there was merit in the view that there had been 'no winners or no losers'. For the assurance of Northern Unionists came a declaration by the Irish Government that 'there could be no change in the status of Northern Ireland until a majority of the people of Northern Ireland desired a change in that status'. This declaration and one by the British Government supporting 'the wishes of the majority of the people of Northern Ireland' were to be registered at the United Nations, an important guarantee. The Conference also agreed that a Council of Ireland would be set up, comprising a Council of Ministers, with a Consultative Assembly having advisory and review functions. This last point was to prove fatal to Faulkner, providing his opponents with 'foot-in-the-door' fear-raising slogans and rumours.

For Faulkner the issue was clear: the Council was non-threatening. On the contrary, viewed against the all-important constitutional guarantees and combined with the unanimity principle in decision taking, he saw the Council as promising much on all-island concerns. Security, social and economic cooperation and relations with Europe were some of the inviting aspects of Sunningdale. Faulkner's opponents would not listen; the General Election shortly to come became a referendum on the Council of Ireland with every 'sign post' reading: 'Dublin is only a Sunningdale away'. Anti-Sunningdale candidates took eleven of the twelve Westminster seats – Gerry Fitt being the only pro-Executive member returned. The result was a devastating blow to the partnership administration; it effectively destroyed the legitimacy of Faulkner's electoral mandate. From then on it was to be downhill all the way for the Chief Minister and his government.

In a more relaxed and trustful situation the agreement made at Sunningdale might have passed into operation without much fuss. But constitutional challenges to its validity in the Dublin High Court, controversy over the meaning of key clauses, continued IRA violence, and the sweeping victory for anti-Sunningdale candidates in the Westminster General Election of February 1974 put a difficult question mark over the interpretation and implementation of the Agreement. Nevertheless, the constitutional reality of partnership was given official confirmation on 31 December 1973. Direct Rule ended and Arthur Brian Deane Faulkner was sworn in as Chief Minister of Northern Ireland's first community government. He appreciated the historic nature of the occasion. Along with his colleagues he knew the risks and he took his stand: 'We stand here of our own free will in a partnership which seeks to face the realities of life in Northern Ireland today. Can anyone doubt that if this Province is to have good government, we must turn aside from our old divisions. I believe not only that what we are engaged upon is right, but that there is no alternative to it.

I say to the people of Northern Ireland: give this administration the chance to work, as it can, and I believe we can employ more power to do good in Northern Ireland than any of our predecessors.'

From January to May 1974, Faulkner and his inter-party Ministry demonstrated their ability to make Protestant and Roman Catholic partnership a reality. For all concerned, it was a unique but short-lived experience; it deserved a better chance. But the decision of the Sunningdale Conference to associate the great adventure of partnership with a controversial 'Irish dimension' required the new Executive to pioneer too much too quickly. On 15 May a general stoppage in opposition to the Council of Ireland was called by the Ulster Workers' Council and before long the Province was heading for total collapse. The final blow came with the UWC demand that the army should assume responsibility for all services. It was a chilling request; the lurch into the unknown feared by the civil authorities had begun. Not only the Executive, the State itself was in danger.

At this point, Faulkner, sensing the magnitude of the crisis, announced that he was not prepared for any political reason to see the country destroyed. He resigned on 28 May, giving both sides an opportunity to retreat with honour. The response was dramatic. By next day the strike had ended – a bewildered Province, never quite at ease with what it had done, settled down to pick up the pieces.

The debate on the reasons for the fall of Northern Ireland's first and only power-sharing Government has continued ever since. Had Faulkner been let down by the British Government? The majority were against the proposed Council of Ireland, but not against power-sharing? Was Merlyn Rees given the support he needed from Downing Street and his military advisers? Were members of the civil service divided in their loyalties?

Much goodwill died in the plethora of recrimination which followed the downfall of the Executive and many of the wounds were long-lasting. But the idea of power-sharing between Protestant and Catholic, Planter and Gael, did not die – it has lingered on, a reminder that there *is* another and better way of doing politics.

For a few months in 1974 Ulster had seen the future – and it worked.

For Brian Faulkner, too, there was no doubt. In answer to a message which I sent him in 1976 he replied:

Highlands
Seaforde, Co. Down
17th September 1976

Dear David,

Thank you very much for a thoughtful, generous, and kindly letter. I worried for a long time before taking my decision but I am convinced it was the right thing to do. I have gone through many sets of negotiations with a series of British Governments and, even if some new initiative were in the offing, and it is not, I just could not see myself going over all the same questions yet again. So, although I have known frustration I have also known satisfaction. I believe that any sacrifice I may have made, to bring about a recognition of partnership and the need for it, was small by comparison with the actual achievement of such co-operation. If only we had been allowed to continue in 1972 we could have shown that our Ulster Cabinet worked well with members of several Parties in it.

David, it has been pleasant to work with you and challenging to see you across the floor!

All regards,

As ever,

Brian

Brian Faulkner, once Ulster's most controversial politician, had the courage to become its most ecumenical leader. He died in a hunting accident on 3 March 1977, mourned in every Province of Ireland.[1]

REFERENCES AND NOTES

1 Bleakley, *Faulkner* (Mowbray, 1974, see Chapter 10 for further details on Power-Sharing Executive).

PART SIX

PRELUDE TO ANGLO-IRISH AGREEMENT

CHAPTER **14**

Lost Decade, 1975–1985

Before its next 'big initiative' Northern Ireland had to endure a decade of painful gestation. Such prolonged periods of waiting were nothing new: since 1969 Ulster people have had to get used to a plethora of stop–go policies, crisis management exercises, democracy by direct rule and, equally debilitating, a gradual take-over by quango-protected government appointees. To add to the democratic deficit, the Executive arm of the State has been permitted to govern without local oversight by a forum of elected representatives – Lord Hailsham's nightmare of an overweening autocracy has come to pass! This is bad for Ministers; it is bad for the Province; and it is also bad for a people who need a parliamentary training ground from which future leaders may be drawn. For all its faults, the old Stormont was strong on parliamentary procedure. Indeed, for many years it was paid the compliment of being used as a tutorial centre for courses provided by the Commonwealth Parliamentary Association.

Certainly there was no shortage of subjects for parliamentary scrutiny in the decade under review. There was, for instance, a crying need for a local parliamentary analysis of the 1974 Ulster Workers' Council (UWC) strike which changed the course of history and which in its implications caused concern to governments worldwide. Robert Fisk in his impressive analysis of the strike (The Point of No Return – the strike which broke the British in Ulster) focused the minds of many with his penetrating conclusion:

> The strike held deep and longterm implications for Britain and other democracies which depend upon social consensus and complex technology to maintain their standard of living. For the Ulster Workers' Council represented something quite new in post-war society: civil disobedience of the most successful and yet most sinister

kind. It undermined the authority of the state broadcasting service; it demonstrated the very patent inability of the trade unions to control their own members; it turned the middle classes against their natural allies, the machinery of administration; and persuaded some of the largest companies in the land to negotiate directly with an unconstitutional junta of militant strikers. It proved the almost total impotence of the army, the police, and of the public authorities; of the civil service; of moderate politicians and – not least – of a frequently insensitive socialist government.[1]

In a telling comparison with other opponents of the State, Fisk observes: 'The Provisionals may have pushed the British into a compromise, but it was the UWC that broke the Labour Government's will to resist.'

Those of us who were members of the Northern Ireland Assembly at the time were well aware of the gravity of the challenge to the state. In the adjournment debate on 21 May (one week before the Executive collapsed) I spoke of the situation in my own shipbuilding constituency of East Belfast:

> Those of us who live in the Greater Belfast area are well aware that the community is on the slide very rapidly. It is true that we have had five years of crisis, but there are ingredients in the present crisis which represent a qualitative change. The kind of difficulties we have faced in the past four of five years are nothing like the potential now building up. We are not confronted by a strike; we are on a collision course between a community and the state. There is a new logic of numbers, a new precision in the crisis and also there is a new impetus. As well as that, the State of Northern Ireland – indeed the United Kingdom generally – has never had to deal with this kind of crisis in a highly sophisticated community.[2]

My point was taken by many investigative journalists and government officials who flooded in from all over the world to see for themselves the way in which, practically without a shot being fired, government could be brought to a standstill in an integral part of the United Kingdom and of the EEC. 'Could it be repeated elsewhere', was the question constantly put to me, especially by observers from Eastern Europe and the former Soviet Union. It was still some years away from 1989, but those to whom I spoke were anxious to learn from our experience. Certainly for months to come those of us with knowledge of strike strategy were much on call in lecture halls and TV stations. But most people in Northern Ireland did not wish to intellectualize about the strike; they were simply glad to get the disruption over and done with. Candles were put away and the electricity came on again; petrol, fast disappearing, resumed its steady flow; and the road barricades, with their threatening self-appointed vigilantes, became a thing of the past. Most Ulster people had sensed that they were getting into very deep water, but did not know how to get out of it. Faulkner's resignation gave them their chance to call it a day. With a collective sigh of relief and, without waiting to be told, people hurried back to work; very soon it was business as usual.

Significantly, those who led the UWC strike played little part in the follow-up political process. No Ulster Lech Walesa emerged to establish a new system of government. On the contrary, little was heard of the UWC as a political factor thereafter. Perhaps Merlyn Rees was correct in his assessment: 'Now that the Executive had broken, I was sure that the strike was going to end and that the coalition of workers and politicians would not last. The UWC had served the politicians' purpose and was now expendable.'[3]

Many lessons were to be learned from the UWC strike, not least by the United Kingdom Government which in future would be more alert in similar circumstances. When Roy Mason came to serve as Secretary of State, he 'saw off' even Mr Paisley; no doubt he had been well advised by his predecessor. 'And what a debriefing Merlyn Rees must have had by Whitehall and the Intelligence Service', I often speculated! But for Secretary of State Rees, too, the strike was a brutal learning experience. He was feeling his way in unknown territory and he was not alone. He and the rest of us were facing elemental forces very different from any which had emerged from the Northern Ireland crisis to date. For reasons such as these it was a pity that Northern Irish politicians had no local forum in which to debate the strike which *nearly* broke the British in Ulster.

An equally emotive community eruption which concerned the Province during the lean years following the resumption of Direct Rule in 1974 was the Hunger Strike by IRA prisoners. Pursued initially as a demand for personal clothes wear in prison, the campaign eventually developed into a strike-to-death demonstration, leading to burial after burial and an emotional wave of grief and concern concentrated in the Catholic community. These events dominated much of public debate and generated considerable street violence throughout the 1980s. Like the Protestant community during the UWC strike, many Catholics felt a sense of grievance and disorientation as a result of the campaign. As one observer in Catholic Derry put it, the hunger strikes 'articulated a tribal voice of martyrdom, deeply embedded in the Gaelic, Catholic nationalist tradition.'[4]

Each phenomenon in its own way, the workers' strike and the hunger strikes, triggered off new waves of alienation in the communities which gave them birth. But in cross-community contacts during and after these campaigns I sensed that, deep down, each community knew also that there were limits beyond which they could not go in pursuit of their leaders' demands – they were prepared to disrupt the family home, but not to destroy it altogether. So, when the time came, community pressures, especially those of the mothers, were effective. As with the UWC the organizers of the Hunger Strike were persuaded to accept, with dignity, something less than victory. Each community was demonstrating to the other that, provided the terms were honourable, it was willing to pull back from the brink. A collective strategy for reconciliation was seeping in.

Such was the situation which confronted Garret FitzGerald when he was elected Taoiseach in 1982. He was deeply disturbed by the state of Anglo-Irish relations which he described as 'little short of disastrous', and he was equally alarmed by the signs of drift towards Sinn Fein in the North. The IRA had capitalized politically on the Hunger Strike, and their Sinn Fein supporters with a new policy of the 'ballot paper and the armalite' were beginning to win seats at local and parliamentary levels. All factors which, he feared, would harm the position of John Hume and his SDLP colleagues – there has always been a rather obvious 'special relationship' between Dublin Governments and the SDLP, often to the despair and detriment of other Northern political groups. In FitzGerald's opinion a new start had to be made to recapture centre stage.

Mrs Thatcher, who had suffered from a great deal of nationalist criticism because of her resistance to concessions during the Hunger Strike, was responsive to FitzGerald's overtures. Unlike FitzGerald and other Southern leaders, she had no real favourites in Ulster politics and felt free to take her own initiatives. Already she had explored with FitzGerald's predecessor, Charles Haughey, the possibility of Anglo-Irish discussions on the 'totality of relationships within these islands', so there was essentially nothing novel in continuing the dialogue with a new Taoiseach. But Garret FitzGerald had a much less traditional vision of nationalism – he thought in terms of a 'New Ireland' with true parity of esteem between North and South. It was all part of what he often described as his 'constitutional crusade' – though, as he discovered later, he had a long way to go before his 'crusade' would look 'crusading' enough for the majority of Northerners to take it seriously.

Before Garret FitzGerald felt free to promote new Anglo-Irish relationships, however, he proposed to stimulate an island-wide dialogue on possible futures for Britain and Ireland. He had already explored some of these 'futures' in his 1982 Richard Dimbleby Lecture and had urged his London audience to face up to realities which had long been recognized in Northern Ireland, but less so in the Republic or in England – like, for instance, the long-standing self-evident truth that the 'free consent of a majority of the people of Northern Ireland' must be central to any real agreement with the North. FitzGerald, with his deep understanding of the North, always seemed ready to go the 'other mile' in his search for reconciliation.

But before FitzGerald became more definitive about the shape of things to come he decided to set up in Dublin in 1983 a New Ireland Forum to consider 'the manner in which lasting peace and stability could be achieved through the democratic process and to report on new structures and processes through which this object might be achieved'. Invitations were generously distributed, though not widely enough accepted, to democratic groups on an island-wide basis.

By any standard the Forum was an impressive gathering. It held eleven public meetings in Dublin and several inter-party discussions in London. In composition it was largely Roman Catholic as Unionist supporters by their self-imposed absence excluded themselves from the debate. As a result many radical Northern options for the future did not get the in-depth examination they required. The general Northern verdict was that the Forum had a 'green' tinge about it – what a pity that those who thought so did not attend and put their case.

However, inside the limitations imposed by composition, the discussions were wide-ranging and the written submissions by 317 groups and persons have provided a well-stocked bank of ideas for the future. Notably, too, this island-wide assembly, largely nationalist in composition, recognized the 'consent' principle for the North.

Most important of all, though, was the conclusion of the Report: 'Accordingly, in the search for the basis of a political solution the British and Irish Governments must together initiate a process which will permit the establishment of common ground between both sections of the community in Northern Ireland and among all the people of this island.'[5] Like many, I looked for more recognition that bilateral talks are no substitute for triangular discussions, London–Dublin–Belfast. 'Ulster a colony once again, but now lorded over by London *and* Dublin,' said many Northerners!

However, it *was* a grand design, promising much; it was also a conclusion which, more than any other consideration, brought together Prime Minister Margaret Thatcher and Taoiseach Garret FitzGerald in the controversial but mould-breaking Anglo-Irish Agreement of 1985. At last, it seemed, the lean years might come to an end.

REFERENCES AND NOTES

1   Robert Fisk, *The Point of No Return* (Andre Deutsch, 1975, p.235).
2   N.I. Assembly Report, 21 May 1974.
3   Merlyn Rees, *Northern Ireland – a Personal Perspective* (Methuen, 1985, p.88).
4   Paul Bew and Gordon Gillespie, *Chronology of the Troubles, 1968–1993* (Gill and Macmillan, p.141).
5   *New Ireland Forum Report* (Stationery Office, Dublin, 1984, p.7).

CHAPTER 15

Anglo-Irish Agreement (and Disagreement), 1985

THOSE IN ENGLAND who make political calculations about Ireland do well to remember the bemusement of Major Sinclair Yeates in *The Experiences of an Irish R.M.* when he tried to understand what was going on about him: 'Major Yeates . . . left his regiment and England equipped with a feeling heart and the belief that two and two inevitably make four, whereas in Ireland two and two are just as likely to make five, or three, and are still more likely to make nothing at all.'[1]

Mrs Thatcher must have felt some of Major Yeates' bewilderment as she tried to reconcile the conflicting interpretations put on her motives for introducing the Anglo-Irish Agreement to Northern Ireland in 1985. Try as she might, the British Prime Minister could not make things 'add up' to the majority of her supporters in Northern Ireland – she understood the simple arithmetic, but not the higher calculus of Irish politics. For FitzGerald, her companion in the partnership, things were better – he had prepared his ground beforehand and had ensured a strong constituency of support.

Mrs Thatcher was quite sure of her intentions and always claimed that she went into the Agreement because she was not prepared to tolerate a situation of continuing violence. In her opinion Garret FitzGerald had got all the glory while she had got the problems! And problems they became: her valued Parliamentary Secretary, Ian Gow, resigned and unrest swept through Unionist and Conservative ranks. This was especially so in Northern Ireland where the Agreement became as damaging to her reputation as did her ill-fated poll tax legislation.

Yet at one level there was much in the new Agreement that must have looked reasonable on the political drawing boards of Downing Street. In statements issued by the British Government *after* (disastrously not *before*) the signing by Prime Minister Margaret Thatcher and Taoiseach Garret FitzGerald at Hillsborough, Co. Down, on 15 November 1985, it was declared that: 'both Governments believe "that the Agreement offers a unique opportunity for Northern Ireland to break away from division and violence, and to make real progress towards peace and stability"'. Three main areas were identified:

1 **The Status of Northern Ireland**. Here firm guarantees are given. Under the Agreement the UK and Irish Governments enter into new and binding commitments: both Governments agreed that any change in the status of Northern Ireland would only come about with the consent of a majority in the Province: and that at present a majority do not want such a change.

   The signatories also pledge that the Agreement will, when it has been approved by the United Kingdom and Irish Parliaments, be lodged at the United Nations. The recognition given in it of Northern Ireland's status will be formally binding in international law – an important safeguard for the Province. Both Governments also undertake that, should a majority in Northern Ireland ever formally consent to the establishment of a United Ireland, then they will support the necessary legislation to bring this about.

2 **Increased Cooperation** between North and South is promised in three crucial areas: the fight against terrorism; economic, social and cultural matters; and the promotion of reconciliation and respect of the two main traditions in both parts of Ireland. The British Government regards increased cooperation in these areas as a gain for all the people of Northern Ireland.

3 Also proposed is an **Intergovernmental Conference** consisting of UK and Irish Ministers, in which the Irish Republic can put forward views on a range of political, security and legal matters. These will include human rights, electoral arrangements, the use of flags and emblems, the avoidance of discrimination, relations between the security forces and the minority, confidence in the administration of justice, extradition and prisons. It is hoped that the Conference, by offering the Republic a voice on those aspects of the Province's affairs that particularly affect the nationalist community, will encourage the minority to identify more closely with the institutions of Northern Ireland.

   The Conference will have a small secretariat of UK and Irish officials: but will have no decision-making powers. The Government will consider the views that the Republic puts forward on behalf of the nationalist community, and will try to resolve any differences.

But actual authority over the affairs of the Province remains with the UK Government and Parliament.

This important section proved the most controversial of the Agreement's proposals and many Unionists regarded the Conference as a revamped version of the Council of Ireland.

On security 'the Intergovernmental Conference is pledged to consider practical ways of improving cross-border operations and to improve relations between the security forces and the nationalist community. But it will not have any operational responsibilities. Responsibility for the RUC will remain with the Chief Constable, and responsibility for the UDR will remain with the General Officer Commanding.'

Devolution – on this question the Government was 'firmly committed to the establishment of a devolved administration in Northern Ireland acceptable to both sides of the community. Nothing in the Anglo-Irish Agreement will impede this. Indeed the Irish Government has declared its support for devolution, and the Agreement allows it to put forward views on how it might be encouraged. The Agreement makes it clear that the Conference would not consider any matters that had been devolved to a local administration.'

On Local Consultation 'the Government promised to continue to seek, value and take into account the views of all local constitutional parties and politicians, including the Northern Ireland Assembly, on all matters affecting the Province. The Anglo-Irish Agreement would not in any way prevent or discourage this. In taking decisions, the Government would be guided by:

– *all* the advice it receives;
– its commitment to respect and recognise both traditions in Northern Ireland;
– the need to reconcile the two traditions.'

The Government concluded that: 'The Anglo-Irish Agreement is a threat to no one but the terrorists. It represents a great chance for the people of Northern Ireland to put behind them the division and violence that has bedevilled the Province for far too long. The Government hopes that all people of sense and goodwill in the Province will welcome it as a basis on which to work together, and build a better future for Northern Ireland.'[2]

By the reckoning of many who value the Union this was a potential starting point for reconciliation within Northern Ireland and between North and South. That is how I saw the Agreement in November 1985 and I said so at the time. But I believed, too, that the North should have a strong presence at the Conference table and hoped that Northern politicians collectively would make their case. I pleaded also for London and Dublin to be even-handed in their dealings with Northerners, Protestant and Catholic alike, and not to be afraid of making the North an equal partner in discussions to do with North–South relations.

Others were less sanguine than I was. The Unionists (Official and DUP) were united in fury. In a joint 'Call to Action', leaders Jim Molyneaux and Ian Paisley saw Secretary of State Tom King as being 'intent on forcing Ulster down the Dublin Road', and called on their followers 'to demonstrate beyond doubt that we will not be trampled on in this manner and that in no circumstances will we ever accept Dublin Rule'.

Strong stuff, sure to confuse and alarm the community. There was more in the same fear-arousing vein: 'This Agreement is a blueprint for an All-Ireland and as such must meet with unrelenting opposition from every Unionist. It cannot be reformed; it must be destroyed.'

On the basis of such extravagant assessments an 'Ulster Says No' campaign was mounted which disrupted Local Government and relations with Northern Ireland Ministers for many years. Only recently has the campaign petered out – it achieved nothing worthwhile and greatly weakened participatory politics in the Province. In particular, 'Ulster Says No' strengthened the already over-strong and overbearing influence of ideologically motivated London Ministers on the shared and valued cultural and social fabric of the Province.

But fear-creation has always been a powerful force in Irish politics and many intrinsically good, though humanly flawed, initiatives have been cut short before being given an adequate testing time – the all-important element of trust has, too often, been missing. As a result, both sides have been unwilling to 'wait and see', while the initiative is mutually explored. So it proved in Northern Ireland in November 1985; following the publication of the Anglo-Irish Agreement, fear swept the Province as all the apprehensions of post-Sunningdale were resurrected. Those who worked in the peace movement, and particularly in the Churches, tried without much success to stem the tide of apprehension. An incident in my own affairs illustrates the difficulty of our task.

In 1985 I was Chief Executive of the Irish Council of Churches and, along with Monsignor Michael Ledwith of Maynooth College, co-Secretary of the prestigious Irish Inter-Church Meeting, which undertook ecumenical work through Ireland. So, as a layman, I was often invited by radio and television to comment on Christian concerns of the day. Such an invitation came in November 1985 when I was asked by Ulster Television to do the popular 'Witness' three-minute talk on their late-night religious 'spot'. This, I thought, was providential timing – a chance to make a Christian appeal for calm at a difficult moment in our affairs. Consultations with my Church brethren confirmed my plans for the broadcast.

I took as my theme the unnecessary fears associated with Halley's Comet, just then on one of its seventy-five-yearly visits close to Earth. I pointed to the comet as a harbinger of false fears which Ulster should reject. Ulster Television's producer and back-up team were enthusiastic about the programme and it was recorded ready for broadcast. On the night in question Church groups were alerted throughout Ireland and we settled down in our various settings to listen together. An interesting group had gathered in our own home: leading Ulster peacemaking activists and, from overseas, Gabi Habib of the Middle East Council of Churches; Jean Fischer, General Secretary of the Conference of European Churches; and, from Germany, Dr Eberhard Spiecker, promoter of the important 'Duisburg Peace Process' initiative to Ireland.

But our gatherings were in vain! At the appointed hour up on our screens flashed the 'Witness' Programme introduction caption, but nothing more! Instead a sober announcement: UTV and the IBA had decided that such a broadcast was not suitable in a religious programme and was therefore held to contravene the Broadcasting Act. By some convoluted misreading of theology my message did not fit the TV establishment view of what was religious! I was 'blacked out' and never again asked to join the 'Witness' team. Apparently they had never heard that modern Christians often witnessed with the Bible in one hand and today's newspaper in the other.

But I had the satisfaction of going out on a high note: my banned broadcast was recognized as a rare event in religious broadcasting and as a result was published far and wide by other sections of the media. For the record, and as an example of the state of tension in 'Halley's-time Ulster' 1985, I share the short script:

Text of Bleakley's blacked-out Broadcast

General Secretary of the Irish Council of Churches, Mr David Bleakley, has released the full text of his broadcast for the religious programme Witness which was taken off the air by Ulster Television last Friday. It was held to contravene a section of the Broadcasting Act. The text is:

'That was a picture of Halley's Comet – something we see every 75 years or so. It's a marvellous sight. And yet, you know, for over 2,000 years that comet has been blamed for every disaster under the sun.

But, of course, the truth is that some pretty good things have also happened when the comet appeared. It came, for instance, in 66AD when Roman soldiers were ravishing Palestine, but at the very same time Christian leaders were spreading the good news of Jesus Christ.

Or, centuries later, when Europe was being laid waste by Attila the Hun, here in Ireland St. Patrick could look up from his great ministry as the comet swept by.

And it's much the same today. The Doomsday Brigade are still with us, booming out their forecasts of bad times. And, the very words of fear they use could become our ruination.

Fear, you see, is the political business of some people. And it's a dangerous thing. As General Eisenhower used to say, "You can't think straight when you're frightened stiff."

But the real danger of the Doomsday Brigade is not only that they would bankrupt us, but that they would have us at one another's throats – Protestant against Protestant and finally Protestant against Catholic. And what a field day that would be for all those who get their evil kicks from sectarian strife. What a legacy to burden our children with – the start of a new Dark Age.

But we are not living in the Dark Ages and we don't have to be blustered into fear and strife. Indeed, the reverse is true. There's plenty to build on if only we do it together.

And that's what we need now in Northern Ireland – a politics of doing things together, because at the end of the day there's nobody else to help us. For instance, do Catholics really believe that Dublin will solve our problems; or can Protestants seriously expect London to bail us out if we allow ourselves to be talked into anarchy?

And that's why the political "guldering" has got to stop. From now on, we have got to put our case in words and actions that will win us friends at home and abroad.

I know it won't be easy, but we can do it if we learn to trust one another, if we learn to forgive, if only somehow we realise that true peace starts when the hating stops.

So, don't be put off by that Doomsday Brigade. Neither they nor Halley's Comet are in control of Ulster's real destiny. The comet will be here again in 2060. Let's make certain that Ulster's grandchildren will be able to look up in pride and prosperity from a truly united Northern Ireland.'

Belfast Telegraph, 1 December 1985

Such for me personally was one of the consequences of the Anglo-Irish Agreement of 1985; but it was a consequence which I was proud to bear.

REFERENCES AND NOTES

1   David Bleakley, *Faulkner* (Mowbray, 1974, p.1).
2   See Appendix VII for further details.

CHAPTER 16

Anglo-Irish Agreement – Postscript

THE ANGLO-IRISH AGREEMENT OF 1985 was an historic milestone in Belfast–London–Dublin relationships – not for what the Accord achieved, but for the redefinition of relationships which it encouraged. There was, for instance, the clear recognition that British/Irish affairs are inseparably intertwined and that they must be pursued together on a basis of parity of esteem. So, for the first time in 800 years, the colonial link between the islands moved towards a sharing of common concerns, publicly recognized. The Anglo-Irish Agreement was a first fruit of that historic realization – historic because it dismantled a centuries-old relationship based on suspicion, conquest and confrontation.

There was a ring of grand design in the joint declaration of November 1985:

* to develop our unique relationship as friendly neighbours
* to diminish divisions in Northern Ireland
* to recognize both traditions
* to reject violence
* to seek a participatory society in Northern Ireland, based on partnership in government.

Plus the promise that any change in the status of Northern Ireland can only come about 'with the consent of a majority of the people of Northern Ireland'. Considerable steps, indeed.

Why then the massive objections to the Accord from within the pro-Union community in Northern Ireland?

Some of the objections arose simply because of the insensitive way in which the Agreement was negotiated and published. No real consultation took place with elected representatives and, in the event, the Agreement was released to press and radio before public representatives were informed. Myself a Privy Councillor, I knew nothing of the announcement until a local reporter telephoned. John Major seems determined to avoid the secretive style of his predecessor; his statements, notably that in Belfast (21 October 1994), have done much to assure the citizens of Northern Ireland that they will not be kept in the dark.

And, as if to underline the lack of sensitivity to local opinion, foci for dissent were encouraged. For example, the headquarters for the controversial new intergovernmental machinery was centred in loyalist East Belfast, requiring access by helicopter or heavily guarded vehicles to avoid predictable demonstrations of protest. These proved many and persistent.

Then, too, the subsequent agenda gave the impression that the only items of injustice worthy of consideration were those involving Northern intransigence. Surely, locals asked, it would be reasonable to assume that there were some areas of injustice in the Republic (or even in England!) which affect the 'friendly neighbour' relationship and which might also be placed on the agenda. A 'parity of esteem issue' was here involved and which required a united Ulster approach – bilateral approaches inevitably assumed that the problems that mattered were only those originating in and emanating from North Ireland.

Nor should such reactions have been unexpected. Ulster has been increasingly distanced from Britain over the past seventy-plus years. The convention of non-interference by Westminster between 1921 and 1969 had much to do with this distancing; and in the years of Direct Rule many examples of insensitivity to the Northern Ireland situation have underlined the difficulty of reversing the process.

In fact, a new relationship (not yet fully recognized by the Westminster or Dublin Governments and only beginning to be sensed by the North Irish) has developed between Belfast and London on the one hand and Belfast and Dublin on the other. The North of Ireland has acquired a new status, requiring recognition. Or, to put it another way, just as it is impossible to visualize a return to a colonial relationship between London and Dublin, so it is impossible to contemplate any constitutional re-arrangement which hints at domination – however slight – by a Dublin Parliament over the North Irish people in their increasingly shared common responsibilities. Close cooperation there must certainly be, but between equals.

Fortunately, since 1972 with the imposition of Direct Rule, a growing number of top politicians at Westminster have had ministerial experience of Northern Ireland and, though there is still a tendency in Britain to simplify the 'Irish Question', increasingly the tendency is being counterbalanced by a realism born out of hard experience of political life in the Province.

But, perhaps just as surprising (and particularly to those who live outside Ireland), there is clear evidence that citizens in the Republic are no longer anxious to become deeply involved in the affairs of Northern Ireland; they are willing to help as good neighbours, but beyond that they are cautious. Nor is this surprising; it is only a measure of the way in which the two parts of Ireland have drifted apart since Partition. Social and economic concerns, the impact of new generations and a greater European involvement – all these have intensified the process.

Of course the myth has been maintained that the South has a deep commitment to Northern Nationalists. The fact of the matter is that Dublin and London have a great deal in common where Northern Ireland is concerned and share a convergence of view more often than they care to admit. Each would like to be rid of the problem, if they could have it so with honour.

And Irish–British colleagueship inside both the United Nations and the EC, and through the apparatus of diplomacy, has greatly reinforced the tendency to look at Northern Ireland as a sort of wayward relative for whom reluctantly they have a shared responsibility.

It is even to be doubted whether the South any longer really wants a 'United Ireland' in any pre-1920 sense of the term. Over seventy years of the South's 'going it alone', changes in the social and economic structure of the two parts of Ireland, the lack of pluralism in Southern Irish society, and, above all, the frightening and costly spectacle of post-1969 violence in the North have convinced most citizens of the Republic that they have problems enough without taking on 'the black North'. The attitude is summed up in the well-known Irish political quip: '*Question* – What is the best way to terrify a Dublin politician? *Answer* – Tell him that the North has decided to join the South.'

People in Ireland are well aware of these facts of life – they are less well known beyond the Irish shore. Indeed, many discussions in Britain about Ireland seem to take little account of post-1920 history. In America it is even worse – there, the intellectual 'benchmark' for Irish debate is all too often fixed in the famine period of the 1840s.

Such facts of life call for a recognition of realities as they exist in Ireland today and a setting aside of notions of what is 'natural' for the island. Coupled to this realization is a growing acceptance that there is a very real limit to the ultimate influence which any outsider may have on Ulster affairs. Neither London nor Dublin holds the final key to the crisis; certainly a helping hand is greatly needed, but at the end of the day it is what happens between the Protestant and Roman Catholic communities in Northern Ireland that really matters.

It is for reasons such as these that the limitations (some of them self-imposed) on the success of the Anglo-Irish Agreement of 1985 are to be regretted. The Agreement promised much, but in the absence of trust between the contending parties in Northern Ireland it was difficult to 'deliver'. Key members of the all-island family were not present and at times the spirit of the 'consent' principle was not observed. This was particularly so with regard to consultation; President-to-be Mary Robinson deplored this inadequacy and resigned from the Irish Labour Party in protest.

So the fuller potential of the Anglo-Irish Agreement was not explored. What could have been a most useful piece of constitutional furniture – a three-legged stool – became an unsure base from which one of the legs (the Northern majority) was missing. There was a leg for the British Government, and the Northern minority were well and truly represented by the Dublin Ministers – but no one was regarded by the public at large as speaking for the greater number in the North who support the Union. No new arrangements for inter-island or inter-Irish dialogue should repeat such mistakes. Nor should Northern pro-Union politicians continue a policy of self-defeating abstention. The time has come for Ulster to say 'yes' when invited to defend and explain its case; it is to be hoped that that 'yes' will become more comprehensive in content and expression as community trust increases.

Of this, even at this stage, we can be sure: the three-legged constitutional stool hinted at by the logic of the 1985 Agreement, and more so by the 1993 Downing Street Declaration, has undoubtedly much to offer:

* it would bring reality and credibility to the conference table
* it would diminish the fears based on ill-informed and often mischievous leaks and rumours
* above all, a new and more realistic Agreement would enable a constitutional device of great potential to bring its pressure to bear on an increasingly wide agenda of inter-Ulster, inter-Irish and Anglo-Irish affairs which can no longer find accommodation within the confines of traditional theories of national sovereignty. Certainly, citizenship rights should not depend so finally on which side of the Irish Sea we live. The 1949 Ireland Act pointed the way to the greater flexibility of citizenship required to meet modern realities. The time has come to re-examine and extend the principles of such a sharing across national boundaries in a triple alliance of shared concern, Republic, Ulster and Britain. Anything less than this invites suspicions of colonial attitudes.

Ideally, we should be working towards the creation of a wider British (or Anglo-Celtic) Isles Council which would take account of our five-peoples pattern in a new community of interdependence, making possible a truly dynamic parity of esteem and opportunity. It is against the background of such expanding possibilities that the Anglo-Irish Agreement should be judged. The design of the Agreement was undoubtedly grand, but it was not grand enough. To set the concept aside would be a disaster, but a revision involving the Northern majority in a truly tripartite dialogue and association would give a way into problems of inter-relationships which affect all of us, wherever we live in the small pattern of islands to which we all belong.

By opening up such prospects, Garret FitzGerald and Margaret Thatcher began a much-needed constitutional reappraisal which takes us far beyond the Irish shore. No doubt, they provided much more than they intended – historically, perhaps it was their greatest hour.

PART SEVEN

CLIMAX OF HISTORY

CHAPTER 17

Turning Spears Into Pruning Hooks – Paramilitary Rubicon

AT MIDNIGHT on Thursday 13 October 1994, I spoke at a very special peace rally outside Belfast's City Hall. Along with young people who had grown up in the troubles, some of the long-term workers for peace in Northern Ireland had come together for a symbolic moment of meditation – to pray, sing and reflect about what we had done together in many years of peacemaking. Across Ireland and across the world we knew we were at that moment part of the 'invisible college' from which reconcilers go out in common witness.

The Belfast City Hall site was particularly symbolic. Scene of so many historically divisive 'Ulster says "NO"' campaigns, we were now using the same piece of Ulster earth as the launch pad for a new slogan 'Ulster says "YES"'. And so it proved to be: my short address opening our meditation mentioned the 'Yes' slogan. It was a sound bite homed-in on by the worldwide television and radio reporters who surrounded us. Sky TV, BBC and stations far and wide carried the short message. In return came pledges of solidarity with 'Yes to Peace in Ireland' from every continent.

Ours was a modest gathering, one of many thanksgiving offerings throughout Ireland that night, but it was hard not to feel a sense of history. A new benchmark question had been created. Just as my generation asks the question 'Where were you on the night Kennedy was assassinated?', so I hoped that for today's 'Young Ulster' the benchmark question was likely to be 'Where were you on the night when peace was declared in Ireland on Thursday 13 October 1994?'.

The event which triggered off Ireland-wide celebrations in October 1994 was the eagerly awaited announcement by the Loyalist Military

Command that they would cease all operational hostilities from midnight on Thursday 13 October 1994. The full text of the statement read:

The Loyalist Statement in full:

After a widespread consultative process initiated by representations from the Ulster Democratic and Progressive Unionist Parties, and after having received confirmation and guarantees in relation to Northern Ireland's constitutional position with the United Kingdom, as well as other assurances, and, in the belief that the democratically expressed wishes of the greater number of people in Northern Ireland will be respected and upheld, the CLMC will universally cease all operational hostilities as from 12 midnight on Thursday, 13 October 1994.

The permanence of our ceasefire will be completely dependent upon the continued cessation of all nationalist/republican violence; the sole responsibility for a return to War lies with them.

In the genuine hope that this peace will be permanent, we take the opportunity to pay homage to all our Fighters, Commandos and Volunteers who have paid the supreme sacrifice. They did not die in vain. The Union is safe.

To our physically and mentally wounded who have served Ulster so unselfishly, we wish a speedy recovery, and to the relatives of these men and women, we pledge our continued moral and practical support.

To our prisoners who have undergone so much deprivation and degradation with great courage and forbearance, we solemnly promise to leave no stone unturned to secure their freedom.

To our serving officers, NCOs and personnel, we extend our eternal gratitude for their obedience of orders, for their ingenuity, resilience and good humour in the most trying of circumstances, and, we commend them for their courageous fortitude and unshakeable faith over the long years of armed confrontation.

In all sincerity, we offer to the loved ones of all innocent victims over the past twenty-five years, abject and true remorse. No words of ours will compensate for the intolerable suffering they have undergone during the conflict.

Let us firmly resolve to respect our differing views of freedom, culture and aspiration and never again permit our political circumstances to degenerate into bloody warfare.

We are on the threshold of a new and exciting beginning with our battles in future being political battles, fought on the side of honesty, decency and democracy against the negativity of mistrust, misunderstanding and malevolence, so that, together, we can bring forth a wholesome society in which our children, and their children, will know the meaning of true peace.

Belfast Telegraph, 13 October 1994.

This statement, along with the equally important but much less expansive one from the IRA in August, ensured that both sides of the paramilitary offensive were now prepared to give democratic procedures a chance. Behind that decision lay many years of patient contact-making by various groups on the Loyalist side, notably the low profile Belfast Presbyterian Minister, the Rev. Roy Magee, who for many years had been engaged in preaching a peace message to the gunmen. He was matched in patience by John Hume, well-known SDLP Member of Parliament, who over a considerable period had established a close dialogue relationship with Sinn Fein leader Gerry Adams.

On the Loyalist side, the honour of making the announcement was given to Gusty Spence, described by the *Unionist Newsletter* as: 'Once a gun warrior, he commanded one of the biggest killing machines to mirror the atrocities of the IRA. Years of experience, tempered by a twenty-year sentence for the murder of a young Roman Catholic (which he has always denied) have persuaded him that 3170 killings are enough.'

Spence is undoubtedly a folk hero in the Loyalist community and his conversion to peacemaking is an important guarantee that the cease-fire will hold – the language of the Loyalist statement reflects this guarantee. This conversion possibility among paramilitaries is no new thing in Northern Ireland; down the years I have met many who have turned to reconciliation work after their release from prison. As I listened to Gusty Spence's statement, I recalled meeting him years ago during my visits to prisoners in support of adult education schemes and other welfare facilities which peace groups encouraged. On these visits I began to recognize the post-prison difficulties and possibilities which some of my students might encounter. Letters which I have subsequently received from republican and loyalist former prisoners alike indicate their willingness to make a fresh start; and many have done so with signal success in academic and social service work.

A message which Gusty Spence sent me from prison confirmed me in my long-held view that paramilitaries *can* be persuaded off violence once a greater idea is put in its place. I quote from part of a letter written from Long Kesh prison:

> I was much impressed by your obvious concern and compassion when you visited Long Kesh immediately after the conflagration, and all loyalist – nay all prisoners – have reason to be grateful to public representatives like yourself who do not take cognisance of a person's political affiliation before speaking out.

It is my earnest wish that we in Ulster may soon enter a
peace that will last and we can then pursue legitimate politics.
Then, and only then, will the people be able to determine
exactly who is best qualified to represent them.

Imprisonment can in some cases make one change and
become wise.

Thank you again,

Yours sincerely,

Gusty Spence

It is many years since Gusty Spence wrote that letter to me. He has
grown with the years, as have many of his Republican counterparts. Now
the problem for them and the community is to find ways in which such as
they can be involved in the democratic procedures which lie at the heart
of a free society. It is also important that those who have left violence as a
way of 'point making' should face the challenge of becoming persuaders
and of putting their case to the test of democratic decision. Like the rest
of us, they must be prepared to face the hazards of democracy – to trust
in the ballot and reject the Armalite.

The Loyalist cease-fire had been preceded by an IRA cease-fire some
three weeks earlier. It, too, was the result of many months of internal
debate following the Downing Street Declaration of 1993. Centre stage in
much of this debate was Mr Gerry Adams whose verbal skills have become
the despair of countless politicians and the fascination of the world media.
The lifting of the increasingly senseless broadcasting ban has done much
to fuel the interest in Sinn Fein, but it has also exposed them to a vigour
of interview with which at times they have seemed decidedly uncomfort-
able. They miss the luxury of being able to speak behind an actor's voice!

Not the least of Gerry Adams' success to date has been his ability to
hold together the very loose coalition of republican interests for which he
speaks; whether he commands the authority of Gusty Spence has yet to be
tested. Signs of the coalition tensions in the republican camp are reflected
in the terseness of the cease-fire announcement and in the ambiguity of
attitude shown towards the Downing Street Declaration. Unlike other
commentators, the IRA are not anxious to 'buy into' the Declaration.
Intent on playing down the significance of the Declaration there is a good
deal of code language in their statement.

IRA Cease-fire Announcement, 31 August 1994

IRA Statement

Cease-fire announced

The IRA today announced an unconditional cease-fire beginning at
midnight tonight.

The IRA statement said: 'Recognising the potential of the current situation and in order to enhance the democratic peace process, the IRA will call a cease-fire from midnight Wednesday, August 31. It will be a complete cessation of military operations and all units have been instructed accordingly.'

The statement added: 'Our struggle has seen many gains and advances made by nationalists for the democratic position. We believe we are entering a new situation, a new opportunity, and we note that the Downing Street Declaration is not a solution, nor was it presented as such by its authors.

A solution will only be found as a result of inclusive negotiations. Others, not least the British Government, have a duty to face up to their responsibilities.

In our desire to significantly contribute to the creation of a climate which will encourage this, we urge everybody to approach this new situation with energy, determination and patience.'

Belfast Telegraph, Wednesday, 31 August 1994.

For the Republican community this cease-fire was presented as a great victory. Gerry Adams, helped particularly by the Irish-American lobby, was enabled to broadcast his claims worldwide and the Dublin Government showed its public gratitude. Predictably there were displays of triumphalism in some 'heartland' areas, with a spate of 'Brits go home' and 'RUC out' demands on the police. Shankill Road loyalists saw things rather differently and on a local gable wall a new mural was colourfully painted in huge and grand lettering: 'On behalf of the Loyalist people of the Shankill Road we accept the unconditional surrender of the IRA – [signed] U.V.F.'

Ironically it was a 'beyond reproach Republican', Mrs Bernadette McAliskey (Devlin, M.P.) who most embarrassed and challenged Adams's view of things. On the night following the IRA truce this fiery apostle of 'pure' republicanism poured scorn on the IRA announcement and suggested to Adams that he had gained nothing that was not on offer many years previously at Sunningdale. She has now carried her case to the United States and suggests that Adams, like Michael Collins in the 1920s, has been tricked into accepting (the consent principle) partition. As she put it in October 1994 to a large audience of Irish-Americans: 'I honestly think that they are doing it all over again.'[1] Mr Adams, perhaps wisely, has refused to tangle with the formidable Bernadette McAliskey on such a sensitive matter.

Bernadette McAliskey is both right and wrong. She is correct in her interpretation of what is on offer, but she is wrong in her assessment of what Michael Collins accepted in the 1920s (but did not live to develop) and what the Taoiseach and John Major might yet agree.

But for most people, having achieved a cease-fire was sufficient in itself. Deep analysis of the situation was no longer the order of the day – sufficient to get the violence stopped and to proceed hopefully from that point. As one Ulster housewife wrote to a local newspaper: 'Peace is going to the sales with worries only about money; it is looking at a parked car without wondering what it holds; it is giving one's opinions in mixed company without worrying.' And that about sums it up – for ordinary people in Northern Ireland life had become pretty intolerable. What they now express is a deep longing for an easing of community tensions and a return to some of the quieter patterns of life. Above all, they seek a turning away from violence as a means of promoting change.

It is important that all who engage in the political process in Northern Ireland spell out the 'fine print' of their proposals to such as that house-wife. Already there is much on offer which is reassuring, provided a spirit of honest give-and-take is observed. This is a vital prerequisite for peace in Ireland – historically it has often been absent when needed most. Much depends on how far minority groups are willing to accept a long-term per-suader role, as the people of Ireland, North and South, prepare to repose confidence in the British Prime Minister and the Republic's Taoiseach. What if the Premiers agree a plan unacceptable to the paramilitaries – will ballot-box democracy be respected? That remains a worrying question.

But behind the cease-fire words of argument, there are hopeful signs that the promoters of violence in Ireland are at least on the wane – that even they are learning that there *is* a more promising life beyond the bomb and the bullet. Furthermore, worldwide, they are being given examples of what can be done to bridge seemingly impossible divides. Perhaps more simply there is a coming to mind of the truth of an older Irish saying: 'Victory comes not to those who inflict suffering, but to those who endure it.' The IRA cease-fire statement was cautious and terse in its commitment (no doubt influenced by the fact that it preceded a loyalist announcement), but it did recognize 'the potential of the current situa-tion' and the need to 'enhance the democratic peace process'. Such guarded statements, if followed up by a peaceful alternative agenda of ballot-box politics, could do much to advance the peace initiative. Sinn Fein must match promise with practice; so, too, all other paramilitary groupings must do likewise.

However there is hope in the willingness and anxiety of Sinn Fein to engage in the democratic debate. Equally encouraging is the Loyalist resolve to 'respect our differing views of freedom, culture, and aspiration and never again permit our political circumstances to degenerate into bloody warfare'. The cease-fires are not an end to the Northern Ireland crisis, but they *do* offer the possibility of a new politics in the Province which will enable the emotional and mental log-jam of centuries to be permanently removed. Both main communities begin to realize that, though they have widespread sympathy, ultimately they are on their own.

It is to be hoped that a community marriage is being 'negotiated'. It will not be made in Heaven; nor will it be 'shot-gun'; more likely it will be a case of two old acquaintances who have known each other for a long time and who have decided to do the decent thing and seal the contract.

For some time to come, Mr Adams and increasingly Mr Spence and his colleagues will continue to make a media mark. Much of what they say is new to radio and television and they are assured of a hearing. But, ultimately, message-by-media must give way to round-the-table discussions and debate with party political opponents. Here will be tested the ability to persuade and to learn something about the patience of politics.

This much we can forecast. The Irish people – and it has been a People's Victory – have achieved a situation of non-violence. They are not prepared under any circumstances to permit a return to a politics of violence. A post-peace position has behind it a public consensus which no self-elected group can be allowed to reverse. Peace in Ireland has become an island-wide imperative; it is inconceivable that the Irish people would permit a reversion to barbarism.

The paramilitary cease-fire has all-Ireland support. All that is now asked is that it should continue. The turning of spears into pruning hooks has begun – let nobody hide a tribal spear in the bunch of pruning hooks.

REFERENCES AND NOTES

1 *Belfast Telegraph*, 24 October 1994.
2 Quoted in Bleakley, *Peace in Ulster* (Mowbray, 1972, p.23).

CHAPTER 18

Getting it Right at Last – The Downing Street Declaration

Downing Street Joint Declaration by Prime Minister John Major and Taoiseach Albert Reynolds on 15th December 1993

WHEN THE DOWNING STREET DECLARATION WAS ANNOUNCED by John Major and Albert Reynolds in December 1993, many in Ireland who were looking desperately for a way out of their island-wide crisis must have been tempted to fall back on their most-quoted political philosopher, Edmund Burke, for consolation. Some were reminded of his popular conclusion: 'When bad men combine the good must associate; else they will fall one by one, an unpitied sacrifice in a contemptible struggle.' Those who studied the document in greater detail and who were more cynical may have preferred Burke's other aphorism: 'It is the nature of all greatness not to be exact'!

But for most in Ireland the Downing Street Declaration represented a victory for common sense and the art of politics. A train of events was set off making possible a new consensus in Ireland on a scale never before achieved; of equal importance, the island-wide consensus had worldwide support, particularly in the United States and the European Community.

For once Ireland had been presented with a political programme which was essentially non-divisive and which evoked in every Province another of their rare collective sighs of relief. As is often the case in Ireland, Church leaders articulated the national response. For Cardinal Daly, it was 'historic' and 'a model of balance and fairness between the unionist and nationalist traditions'; Dr Robin Eames, the Church of Ireland Primate of All Ireland, called the Declaration 'courageous' and hoped 'that many will be reassured that their deeper fears have not been realised'; the powerful Government Committee of the Presbyterian Church recognized that the Declaration 'represents a serious attempt by the British and Irish Governments to face up to the realities of an historically complex problem and to attempt to reconcile the parties involved'.

The first hurdles in acceptance were over. Both Dublin and London had learned from previous declaratory initiatives that in politics 'style' in presentation is every bit as important as 'content'.

At a first glance the details of the 1993 Declaration contained little that had not been on offer twenty years earlier. In an identification of important areas the influential *Irish Times* underlined:

The Main Points
The joint declaration:

- will uphold the democratic wish of a greater number of the people of NI on whether they prefer to support the Union or a sovereign united Ireland
- the British have no selfish strategic or economic interest in NI
- the role of the British will be to encourage, facilitate and enable the achievement of agreement
- such agreement may, as of right, take the form of agreed structures for the island as a whole, including a united Ireland achieved by peaceful means
- it is for the people of the island of Ireland alone, by agreement between the two parts respectively, to exercise their right of self-determination on the basis of consent, freely given, North and South, to bring about a united Ireland, if that is their wish
- the democratic right of self-determination by the people of Ireland as a whole must be achieved and exercised with and subject to the agreement and consent of a majority of the people of Northern Ireland.

But underlying the staid language of the Declaration there were many signs that 'space' was being given to all those who wished to pursue legitimate aspirations by democratic means. As Albert Reynolds and John Major together affirmed:

The most urgent and important issue facing the people of Ireland, North and South, and the British and Irish Governments together, is to remove the causes of conflict, to overcome the legacy of history and to heal the divisions which have resulted, recognising that the absence of a lasting and satisfactory settlement of relationships between the peoples of both islands has contributed to continuing tragedy and suffering. They believe that the development of an agreed framework for peace, which has been discussed between them since early last year, and which is based on a number of key principles articulated by the two Governments over the past 20 years, together with the adaptation of other widely accepted principles, provides the starting point of a peace process designed to culminate in a political settlement.

After twenty years of Direct Rule from Westminster, the 1993 Declaration was setting out constitutional principles and political realities which safeguarded the vital interests of both sides of the community in Northern Ireland. It reflected the beliefs of both Governments, but compromised the principles of neither. It claimed to make no prejudgements.

But unlike previous agreements the 1993 Declaration also confronted the paramilitaries and their supporters with a challenge and a choice: give up the use of, or support for, paramilitary violence and accept the responsibility of seeking a democratic mandate which will open the way to full participation in democratic politics. Freedom to join in dialogue between the Governments and the political parties on the way ahead would follow in due course. This proposal won resounding public approval; those who depended on the gun faced complete marginalization as they were confronted with a unique all-Ireland collective consciousness which demanded an immediate and permanent end to violence. Should Sinn Fein or any other group ignore this consensus, they would for the first time in Irish history face the democratic wrath of free peoples whose governments are now mandated and expected to make all of Ireland a common-security island, barred to terrorists. Little wonder that very soon after the Declaration a significant debate began among the armed factions and their political advisers as they pondered the risks.

But the Declaration was about much more than violence. In particular, Mr Reynolds and Mr Major had the courage 'to see old fears and animosities replaced by a climate of peace'. The spelling out of this message represents a historic sea-change in Anglo-Irish relations, climaxing in an agreed statement which accommodates current realities and future changes in a well-balanced package of community-healing proposals.

Much of this 'future tense' thinking has to do with a long-overdue recognition of truths which are self-evident. Ancient myths about Britain and Ireland are at last being publicly questioned at the highest levels. Modern realities are being given pride of place.

For example, there is on offer a declaration of intent which, while no longer insisting that Dublin be given responsibility for Northern Ireland, leaves the door open for an examination of ways in which non-threatening and mutually acceptable forms of North–South cooperation can be developed to the advantage of both Irish jurisdictions. 'And near time, too,' say a growing majority of Irish people of both main traditions. Political pundits who would read significant constitutional implications into such initiatives are increasingly viewed with impatience by most citizens. 'Let's get on with a bit of commonsense cooperation and see what happens', is the more popular and likely-to-prevail view.

On constitutional issues which *do* arise there is an equally pragmatic approach. It has been for long generally recognized by the Irish who live in Ireland, and now confirmed by the reception given to the Declaration, that a growing majority in Northern Ireland has no real interest in either an enforced united Ireland or an independent Ulster. 'A plague on both your houses!' say most Northerners, who simply want the violence to end so that they can get on with the business of rebuilding their battered community. Currently, the shared hope is for agreed structures of regional government, based on responsibility and power-sharing, and meaningful inter-Ireland institutions for cross-border cooperation. Once shared structures of government are in place, Protestants and Catholics together look forward to enjoying a considerable social and economic Peace Bonus.

Above all, and at every stage in the historic Declaration, London and Dublin made it clear that the constitutional future of Northern Ireland is in the hands of its own people. Here again is the recognition of a reality to do with geography, history and population.[1]

Taken together, these assurances give room for the creative expression of both traditions in Northern Ireland, and constitute a threat to neither. It also represents a final setting-aside of uncertainties and suspicions to do with outmoded colonial relationships. So, a new climate is created which uniquely challenges divisive notions of pan-Nationalism and pan-Unionism. Peacemakers look to the emergence of a Pan-People's Front powered by the principles of the 1993 Declaration.

Confidence-building will not be easy, but for the great majority of people in Ireland a new chapter in North–South relations has begun which makes possible the emergence of an agreed Northern Ireland, at peace with itself and at ease with its neighbours. Such is the legacy of the Downing Street Declaration.

This 'feel good' factor was of course a vital component of the Declaration's success. As we have already noted, timing was an important factor – the December 1993 date was not fortuitous. The few years previous had seen the emergence of new men and a new Government in Dublin. Dick Spring, a Labour leader in Foreign Affairs, had greatly raised the profile of reconciliation; his opposite number from Britain, Sir Patrick Mayhew, was equally dedicated and popular across the board. With Taoiseach Reynolds and Prime Minister Major heading the team the political chemistry was complete.

But in the Ireland of 1993, a more fundamental chemistry was at work – the chemistry of the people, North and South, who sensed that they were being led into an Armageddon position by deeply sinister developments on the security front. Not enough attention has been given to this collective consciousness. New strategies of violence were being developed by both main paramilitary groups, involving new targets (personal and propertywise); increasingly the areas of operation lay far beyond the Ulster Province. The 'British mainland' was now also a 'legitimate' IRA target, symbolized most tragically in the Warrington bombing which evoked international outrage. As the *Belfast Telegraph* noted, 8 April 1993: 'Warrington has indeed become England's Enniskillen, bringing new international pressure to bear – the IRA have forfeited all but the fanatical good will.' President Mary Robinson, members of the Royal Family and many international representatives attended the Warrington mourning service. It stirred the nations.

Britain was also called upon to bear an economic war as assaults on railway and air installations were mounted. More drastic, and more expensive financially, there were attacks on the City of London in the 1990s which, long regarded as a safe haven for international business, now began to look desperately vulnerable. 'The Government will have to do something about it' muttered the City – even the gnomes of Zurich and Tokyo were said to have expressed concern!

A chilling Irish addition to this concern was a warning by security chiefs that the loyalists had now reached parity of efficiency and sophistication in weaponry. This became all the more menacing with the announcements that targeting against the 'pan-Nationalist' front was to be introduced – a barbaric descent into universal targeting with horrendous 'tit-for-tat' possibilities. Instinctively, in self-defence, the Northern community began to express a new solidarity against ultimate violence. In the early 1990s this took the form of a growing cease-fire movement which greatly strengthened the pressure on paramilitaries across the board. Something like a long-needed 'Rainbow Coalition' had emerged throughout the Northern Ireland community in respect to an immediate and permanent end to violence.

This Northern solidarity was powerfully reinforced by parallel developments in Southern attitudes. As leading Dublin commentator, Gemma Hussey explains in her powerful analysis, *Ireland Today – Anatomy of a Changing State*[2], the Republic of Ireland has been experiencing its own metamorphosis. In fact, a political 'de-greening' of the Republic has been going on in recent decades; and it has affected attitudes to the North.

As a result, Southern politicians are empowered – indeed required – to break out of their forefathers' diplomatic mould. In Gemma Hussey's judgement 'the results of Ireland's June 1993 election showed a marked acceleration of a trend away from the politics of a finally forgotten civil war towards a younger, more European style of social democracy. Politicians of the old school who failed to appreciate what was going on had paid the price of their blindness. The old guard has passed on.'[3]

Ms Hussey also castigates the Irish old guard in America who are consistently out of touch with contemporary Irish opinion and particularly so with regard to so-called 'Irish freedom fighters' who collect money for 'the cause'. Her scorn is pungent: 'Do they not realise' she asks, that 'Irish Governments have been trying for years to convince Irish-Americans that the IRA are not heroes or freedom fighters, but are held in contempt at home, where under two per cent of the electorate cast their votes for the political allies of the IRA, the Sinn Fein Party?'[4] Such comments are becoming more frequent and more effective in contemporary Irish politics.

The election of Mary Robinson as President of Ireland in 1990 was the clearest completed signal of all that a new Ireland was beckoning. By challenging the Irish political status quo she created a major historical event, and gave hope and courage to a widest-ever constituency. *How* wide I realized when on Election night a Reverend Mother from one of Ireland's most traditional convents telephoned me the news: 'David, all the sisters will be voting for Mary.' At that moment I knew that Mary Robinson was assured of victory.

But in terms of the Downing Street Declaration, Mrs Robinson's election was important because of the modern pluralism it represented. Taoiseach Albert Reynolds now had behind him a President who was herself breaking the mould; her great affection and sympathy for the North enabled him to traverse new ground which his predecessors dared not enter. And her call to the nation gave encouragement to those who shared her vision of a new Ireland: 'I say, take heart. There is hope. Look what you did in this Election. You made history.'

Encouraged by such a Presidential presence Albert Reynolds was free to explore with John Major the totality of Anglo-Irish relations as never before; their Downing Street Declaration of 1993 became an approach in tune with the realities of modern Ireland.

The Downing Street Declaration initiative was completed in February 1995 by the publication of 'Frameworks for the Future', an intergovernmental discussion paper presented by Prime Minister Major and newly elected Taoiseach John Bruton. The document expressed high hopes: 'a new beginning for relationships within Northern Ireland, with the whole of Ireland and between the peoples of these islands'.[5]

All over Ireland the people have indicated that they are prepared to take the leap of faith as Northern Ireland, perhaps for the last time, is being given another chance for communal unity within its boundaries. It is now required of political leaders who negotiate the future that they become part of the liberating sea-change in attitudes which has taken place, island-wide, among their people.

As we in Ireland wait and work for a justly balanced outcome we need more and more to rely on that 'vision thing' – that something extra which will give us the courage to explore together, not as strangers but as pilgrims on a common journey. We need to find a new dimension of trust in one another. Where can it be found?

Perhaps it is most appropriately to be found in the ancient Irish concept of belonging to a Fifth Province which Mary Robinson so well resurrected in her Inaugural Address. For President Mary that Fifth Province has become a special place pointing up the vision of 'an emerging Ireland of tolerance and empathy'. It is an all-island vision, offering true 'space' to affirm our shared affairs and freeing us from past constraints.

Geographically, we in Ireland have been born into conflicting allegiances – sometimes not only in the province of Ulster but in Munster, Leinster and Connaught as well. But wisdom from our ancestors reminds us that a timeless non-geographical allegiance is also available – a place within each of us open to the other, a swinging door which allows us to venture out and enter in. The Presidential Address of Mary Robinson concluded: 'If I am a symbol of anything I would like it to be a symbol of the reconciling and healing Fifth Province.' We need such symbols in Ireland today.

With many others, and for many decades, I have searched for the pollen of peace in Ireland's fields of conflict. Now we know that it can be found in abundance in Ireland's Fifth Province. Let us collect it together.

REFERENCES AND NOTES

1   See Appendix IX for additional material.
2   Gemma Hussey, *Ireland Today, Anatomy of a Changing State* (Townhouse Viking, Dublin, 1993, p.1).
3   Ibid., p.1.
4   Ibid., p.4.
5   See Appendix X: Frameworks for the Future.

Appendices

In these Appendices are brought together a few of the background documents which reflect on issues at the centre of today's Irish debate.

Appendices I–VI – Sectarianism in Ireland

These extracts come from the Report of the Working Party on Sectarianism, set up by the Department of Social Issues of the Irish Inter-Church Meeting (published in 1993 by IICM, Inter-Church Centre, 48 Elmwood Avenue, Belfast). At the Inter-Church Meeting in 1987, Archbishop Robin Eames, Church of Ireland Archbishop of Armagh, and the then Roman Catholic Archbishop of Armagh, the late Cardinal Tomas O'Fiaich, suggested that the Churches needed to examine closely 'the lethal toxin of sectarianism which at times seems almost to have overwhelmed us.' As a result of their lead the Meeting authorized the Working Party's investigation which resulted in a much welcomed and widely discussed Report. Of particular interest are the views of the Churches as they reflect on one another's position.

Appendices

Church Sources

CHURCH SOURCES

APPENDIX I

Segregation of the Communities in Northern Ireland

1) Segregation in Everyday Life

Research based on the 1991 Census[1] has found that half the population now lives in areas that are more than 90 per cent Catholic or Protestant. Segregation is most notable in working class areas of Belfast, parts of Derry, in a few of the smaller towns and some tracts of the countryside.

The onset of the troubles brought enormous upheavals, reversing what had been a gradual trend towards more integration of Protestants and Catholics. **The widespread civil disturbances of the early 1970s led to massive population movement**. Whole areas, which had been mixed, became segregated as one side or the other moved out. Most of the movement took place in Belfast and surrounding housing estates. No one knows how many people fled, but an official estimate was that in the three years from 1969 to 1972 between 8,000 and 15,000 families had been forced to evacuate their homes. **Most of these were Catholic**. However, **one of the features of more recent times has been a marked tendency for Protestants to move away from certain areas** – the west bank of the Foyle, parts of Fermanagh and parts of South Down. **The net result has been an increase of segregation over the last twenty years**. Research based on the 1991 Census found that the number of predominantly Catholic electoral wards in Northern Ireland has almost trebled from 43 to 120 and the number that are almost exclusively Protestant has doubled from 56 to 115.

There is a tendency for there to be **more segregation in the public housing sector than in the private sector**. According to the PSI Report[2] 37 per cent manual Catholic households in Northern Ireland Housing Executive dwellings were in wards where 90 per cent or more of the population were of the same religion; the corresponding proportions for manual households in the private housing sector were 19 per cent and 37 per cent.

However, studies[3] have seemed to suggest that the **degree of everyday separation of Catholic and Protestant is not as pronounced in the small towns and villages of the countryside as it is in working class urban areas**. They have also seemed to suggest that being a Catholic or a Protestant is not as important a consideration for certain activities like visiting or attending funerals and marriages as it is for events which take place in more public areas. Most areas in rural Northern Ireland have managed to maintain a kind of modus vivendi, which encourages people to play down the central religio-politico division in day-to-day life. There are also other forces at work other than the Protestant/Catholic one to bring people together or push them apart, e.g. social class.

It may be that there is a **strong 'particularity of place' in Northern Ireland, each with its own pattern of integration and segregation**. Community relationships may vary quite widely, depending, for instance, on local history, on patterns of economic cooperation and mutual reliance, on geographical factors and local peculiarities, e.g. people being educated together in the local school.

2) Segregation at Work

According to the first monitoring returns produced under the Fair Employment Act 1989[4] 48 per cent of all companies have less than ten employees of one religion or another. Sixty per cent of people in employment work for an employer where there is a significant under representation of one community or another. There is, therefore, **a high degree of segregation in the workplace**.

3) Segregation in Education

It is believed that there is no significant cross-enrolment in the primary school sector, although a small number of primary schools are known to have a religious mix. Overall, voluntary grammar schools, which are not under Catholic management, and controlled grammar schools have just over 5 per cent Catholic pupils and controlled secondary schools just over 2 per cent. The proportion of Protestant pupils enrolled in Catholic schools, grammar or non-grammar schools is insignificant. Planned integrated schools have around 1 per cent of pupil numbers. **There is therefore a very considerable degree of segregation in the education system.**

4) Mixed Marriage

According to a survey by Professor Paul Compton and Dr. John Coward[5] **one in sixteen Northern Ireland marriages are mixed marriages**. In 40 per cent of cases one of the partners changes their religious denomination. Half of the children are brought up as Catholics. Mixed marriage is highest among manual workers and more common in the "more peaceful and less segregated" north coast area of the province and lowest in the "sectarian conflict" areas of mid-Ulster and South Armagh. Mixed marriages have increased since the 1950s and are still rising, although a decline was noted when the troubles were at their height between 1968 and 1972.

5) Voluntary Social Activities

Duncan Morrow suggests[6] that the **Churches are probably the largest providers of social and recreational activities** in Northern Ireland (for instance, only 15 per cent of Churches do not have recreational activities of some kind for young people), but he found that there is **little cross-community participation** except perhaps in bowling clubs. Whyte suggests[7] that segregation varies from area to area and between classes.

References

(1)   Research cited in *The Independent on Sunday*, March 21, 1993.

(2)   David J. Smith and Gerald Chambers, op.cit., pp.20-21.

(3)   H. Donnan and G. McFarland "Continuity and Change in Rural Northern Ireland" in P. Clancy, S. Drudy, K. Lynch and L. O'Dowd (eds.), *Ireland: A Sociological Profile* (Dublin, 1986).

(4)   Fair Employment Commission, *A Profile of the Northern Ireland Workforce: Summary of the Monitoring Returns* (Belfast, 1992).

(5)   Paul Compton and John Coward, *Fertility and Family Planning in Northern Ireland* (Aldershot, 1989).

(6)   Duncan Morrow, op.cit.

(7)   John Whyte, op.cit., p.38.

APPENDIX II

The Roman Catholic Church and the Protestant Churches

I   The Roman Catholic Church and the salvation of non-Roman Catholic individuals
II   The Roman Catholic Church and the salvific role of the non-Roman Catholic Churches
III   The Roman Catholic Church and the defectiveness of the other Churches
IV   The Roman Catholic Church and Religious Freedom
V   The Roman Catholic Church and Ecumenism

I   The Roman Catholic Church and the Salvation of non-Roman Catholic Individuals

I.1   Until the 17th century the Roman Catholic Church tended to hold a rigid interpretation of the dictum "outside the Church no salvation".

I.2.   But the Roman Catholic Church now holds that all who follow Christ can be saved. Indeed it now holds that everyone can be saved, irrespective of religion or Church:

- *We must hold that the Holy Spirit offers to all the possibility of being made partners, in a way known to God, in the paschal mystery.* (Vatican II, *The Church in the Modern World*, par.22).

- *Those who, through no fault of their own, do not know the Gospel of Christ or his Church, but who nevertheless seek God with a sincere heart, and, moved by grace, try in their actions to do his will as they know it through the dictates of their conscience – those too may achieve eternal salvation. Nor shall divine providence deny the assistance necessary for salvation to those who, without any fault of theirs, have not yet arrived at an explicit knowledge of God and who, not without grace, strive to lead a good life.* (ibid., *The Church*, par.16).

II   The Roman Catholic Church and the Salvific Role of the non-Roman Catholic Churches

II.1   Prior to Vatican II the Roman Catholic Church would have been more inclined to hold that Protestants were saved despite their Churches than because of them. The Protestant Churches were regarded more as obstacles than as helps to faith; they were not seen as means of salvation. So it was that the validity of baptism administered by the Protestant Churches was in fact, if not in law, often presumed to be doubtful. So it was that in Ireland during the nineteenth century when fear of proselytism was very great any assistance at an act of worship in a Protestant Church was for a Catholic illicit, a sin and, in places at least a reserved sin. It was not only active participation which was excluded as illicit but also what has been termed material or passive presence, e.g. as a mere act of courtesy or civic duty. And despite changes in the 1917 Code of Canon Law allowing such passive attendance at, for example, weddings and funerals, nineteenth century attitudes lingered on and the obsequies in St. Patrick's Cathedral Dublin in 1949 of Douglas Hyde, first President of Ireland, were not attended by the Taoiseach of the day or the Catholic members of his cabinet.

II.2. Since Vatican II the Roman Catholic Church clearly affirms the salvific role and truly ecclesial character of all the other Churches: they have "significance and importance in the mystery of salvation". (ibid., *On Ecumenism,* par.3).

> *The brethren divided from us also carry out many liturgical actions of the Christian religion. In ways that vary according to the condition of each Church or community, these liturgical actions most certainly can truly engender a life of grace, and, one must say, can aptly give access to the communion of salvation.*
> *It follows that the separated Churches and communities as such ...have been by no means deprived of significance and importance in the mystery of salvation. For the Spirit of Christ has not refrained from using them as means of salvation.* (ibid, par.3).

This recognition of the salvific role of the Protestant Churches means that, for Roman Catholics, prayer in common with other Christians becomes "allowable, indeed desirable" in certain circumstances. It means that worship in common can be used, but "not indiscriminately" as a way of promoting Christian unity. (ibid., par.8).

III. The Roman Catholic Church and the Defectiveness of the other Churches

III.1. The Roman Catholic Church holds that in its eyes, all the other Churches are more or less defective: they "do not profess the Catholic faith in its entirety or have not preserved unity or communion under the successor of Peter" (Vatican II, *The Church* par.15); only through the Roman Catholic Church is the "fullness of the means of salvation" to be attained. (ibid. *On Ecumenism,* par.3). In particular, the orders of the other Churches (with the exception of the Eastern and Old Catholic Churches) are not recognised. Anglican Orders were declared "absolutely null and utterly void" by Pope Leo XIII in 1896.

III.2. But to lack "the fullness of the means of salvation" is not to lack all the means of salvation (cf. above II). The defectiveness asserted is only partial.

III.3. Besides, the defectiveness asserted is simply a structural, institutional defectiveness, a defectiveness at the level of "means"; and "the means of grace", the "means of salvation" cannot be confused with grace itself, with salvation itself.

III.4. Hence the defectiveness asserted in no way implies a spiritual defectiveness. Other Christians are not necessarily less holy. "By his (the Holy Spirit's) gifts and graces, his sanctifying power is also active in them and he has strengthened some of them even to the shedding of their blood". (ibid., *The Church*, par.15). But cf. V.1 below.

III.5. Because of all that is shared (Scriptures, Creeds, the life of grace, etc.) the Roman Catholic Church sees the members of the other Churches as in communion with it but because of the existing structural defectiveness, in a state still of partial, imperfect communion; not yet in full communion. (ibid., *On Ecumenism*, par.3). As a result eucharistic sharing is forbidden except in certain special circumstance with episcopal permission. (ibid., *On Ecumenism*, par.8).

IV. The Roman Catholic Church and Religious Freedom

IV.1. Until Vatican II the theoretical position of the Roman Catholic Church towards those who differed from it was one of toleration based on expediency. Error, it held, had no rights but it was not always practical or possible to suppress error so it could and might be tolerated as the lesser of two evils.

IV.2. On 7 December 1965 the Roman Catholic Church formally recognised that religious freedom was not something to be grudgingly conceded but an intrinsic universal right:

> *The Vatican Council declares that the human person has a right to religious freedom. Freedom of this kind means that all men should be immune from coercion on the part of individuals, social groups and every human power so that, within due limits, nobody is forced to act against his convictions in religious matters in private or in public, along or in associations with others. (Declaration on Religious Liberty, par.2).*

IV.3. The critical importance of Vatican II's Declaration on Religious Liberty was well expressed by the Lutheran theologian and professor at Yale, George Lindbeck:

*Most of us remember the preconciliar situation in which ecumeni-
cal discussions revolved around the issue of religious liberty. Non-
Catholics, perhaps especially in America, were obsessed with the
question of what would happen to civil and religious liberties if
Catholics became a majority. They constantly asked if the Church
approved of the disabilities under which non-Catholics suffered in
places like Spain. This was the end-all and the be-all of most
interchurch exchanges. Ecumenism could not advance under
these circumstances. It was only because of the Declaration on
Religious Freedom ... that the way was opened for the Decree on
Ecumenism.*

(W. J. Burghardt (ed.), *Religious Freedom 1965-1975* (New
York, 1976), p.52.).

V. The Roman Catholic Church and Ecumenism

V.1. Since Vatican II the Roman Catholic Church holds that a divided Church
is intolerable: it "openly contradicts the will of Christ, provides a
stumbling block to the world, and inflicts damage on the most holy cause
of proclaiming the good news to every creature"; it is as if Christ himself
were divided. *(Decree on Ecumenism,* par.1).

V.2. According to Vatican II this scandal of Christian disunity is to be reduced
and overcome by institutional renewal and reform (ibid., par.6), by
cooperation according to conscience (ibid., par.12) and by theological
dialogue. (ibid., par.9).

V.3. Since Vatican II the Roman Catholic Church no longer holds what Pope
Pius XI taught in 1928, i.e. that "there is but one way in which the unity
of Christians may be fostered, and that is by furthering the return to the
one true Church of Christ of those who are separated from it; for from that
one true Church they have in the past fallen away". *(Mortalium Animos).*

APPENDIX III

How the Church of Ireland Views the Roman Catholic Church

1)   *The Thirty-Nine Articles of Religion,* received and approved by the Church of
Ireland, first in 1634 and again in 1870 (at Disestablishment), and to which clergy
taking up their ministry are required to 'assent' refer, in language that reflects
the idiom of their day, to several fundamental matters of doctrine:

> *19. Of the Church.*
> *The visible Church of Christ is a congregation of faithful men, in the*
> *which the pure Word of God is preached, and the Sacraments be duly*
> *ministered according to Christ's ordinance in all those things that*
> *of necessity are requisite to the same.*
> *As the Church of Jerusalem, Alexandria, and Antioch, have erred;*
> *so also the Church of Rome hath erred, not only in their living and*
> *manner of Ceremonies, but also in matters of Faith.*
> *22. Of Purgatory.*
> *The Romish Doctrine concerning Purgatory, Pardons, Worshipping*
> *and Adoration as well of Images as of Reliques, and also invocation*
> *of Saints, is a fond thing, vainly invented, and grounded upon no*
> *warranty of Scripture, but rather repugnant to the Word of God.*
> *31. Of the one Oblation of Christ finished upon the Cross.*
> *The offering of Christ once made is the perfect redemption,*
> *propitiation, and satisfaction, for all the sins of the whole world,*
> *both original and actual; and there is none other satisfaction for sin,*
> *but that alone. Wherefore the sacrifices of Masses, in the which it*
> *was commonly said, that the Priest did offer Christ for the quick and*
> *the dead, to have remission of pain or guilt, were blasphemous*
> *fables, and dangerous deceits.*

According to the "Preamble and Declaration" to the *Constitution and Canons
Ecclesiastical of the Church of Ireland* (adopted by the General Convention of
1870)

> *1.   The Church of Ireland doth, as heretofore, accept and un-*

feignedly believe all the Canonical Scriptures of the Old and New Testament, as given by inspiration of God, and containing all things necessary to salvation; and doth continue to profess the faith of Christ as professed by the Primitive Church.

3. *The Church of Ireland, as a Reformed and Protestant Church, doth hereby re-affirm its constant witness against all those innovations in doctrine and worship, whereby the Primitive Faith hath been from time to time defaced or overlaid, and which at the Reformation this Church did disown and reject."*

2). Since Vatican II in the Roman Catholic Church there has been a gradual evolution of view regarding that Church, and a more eirenic tone of language. The *Revised Catechism,* produced in the early 1970s, says the following:

23. *What should be your attitude to other Christians?*
I should recognise them as my brothers and sisters in Christ and show courtesy and understanding towards them.

In 1975 the General Synod passed the following resolution on the *Thirty-Nine Articles*:

That this House, while not desiring in any way to alter the doctrinal content of the Thirty-Nine Articles but recognising that certain statements therein are regarded as uncharitable, requests the House of Bishops to ask the Anglican Consultative Council to examine such statements with a view to the removal of misunderstanding and the avoidance of language which might be deemed offensive to our fellow Christians of other denominations.

The Church of Ireland, while expressing reservations about aspects of the *Final Report* of the Anglican-Roman Catholic International Commission (ARCIC-I), says (1981) with respect to the Report's "Agreed Statement on Authority in the Church":

Therefore we express our gratitude to the theologians who prepared the Agreed Statement. In many ways it is an admirable Statement. We praise the members of the Commission for trying to avoid old polemics and the emotional language associated with them. The criticisms we make in our response indicate the difficulty of the task to which they have put their hand. The measure of the progress which they have made is a ground for hope and joy, for the Agreed Statement would seem to provide a sufficient theological basis for further official dialogue.

and in its official response to the *Final Report* said (1986):

Meanwhile, the Church of Ireland needs to recommit itself to the goal of visible unity in Faith, Order and eucharistic Fellowship and to redouble its efforts to work with Roman Catholic and other Christian people for that unity which is grounded in truth, love and holiness.

It is important in our search for unity in truth that we continue …to encourage growth in personal and community relationships between members of the Church of Ireland and people of all Christian traditions in Ireland, including those of the Roman Catholic Church.

Roman Catholic regulations with regard to inter-Church marriages have been a source of much Church of Ireland criticism, though it is acknowledged that some steps have been taken to meet Protestant objections. Official responses are still awaited to the *Report of the Anglican Roman Catholic International Commission on the Theology of Marriage and its Application to Mixed Marriages*. Nonetheless the operation of Roman Catholic rules in the Diocese of Ferns, as agreed with the Church of Ireland, demonstrates that substantial advances can be made.

In practical terms, the Churches have officially developed their relationships with one another. For instance, the Church of Ireland, along with other Protestant Churches, has participated in the (Ballymascanlon) Inter-Church Talks with the Roman Catholic Church, which commenced in 1973.

Furthermore, the invitation by the General Synod to the Roman Catholic Church to send representatives to its meetings, (an invitation readily accepted), signifies progress in relations and a new perception of how relations should be conducted.

APPENDIX IV

How the Presbyterian Church in Ireland Views the Roman Catholic Church

The Westminster Confession of Faith

Presbyterians in Ireland find their statement of Christian beliefs enshrined in the *Westminster Confession of Faith* along with the *Larger* and *Shorter Catechisms*. These documents were drawn up by the Westminster Divines of 1646. They are known as "subordinate" standards, by which is meant subordinate to Scripture – for Presbyterians the "supreme" standard for faith and practice. The longest chapter in the *Confession* is given over to "Holy Scripture" and it concludes with the words:

The Holy Spirit speaking in the Bible is the supreme judge of all religious controversies, all decisions of religious councils, all the opinions of ancient writers, all human teachings, and every private opinion. We are to be satisfied with the judgement of Him Who is and can be the only judge.

In the *Westminster Confession of Faith* there are several statements concerning some aspects of Roman Catholic dogma which are regarded as unscriptural and therefore unacceptable.

(1) Presbyterian Understanding of Scripture

Presbyterians only accept the Old and New Testament books (66 in all) as divinely inspired and concerning the Apocryphal books which the Roman Catholic Church accepts says, *"The books usually called Apocrypha are not divinely inspired and are not part of the canon of Scripture. They therefore have no authority in the Church of God and are not to be valued or used as anything other than human writings."* (1:3)

(2) Presbyterian Understanding of Worship

The *Confession of Faith* makes statements concerning the worship of God which are at variance with what are understood to be some Roman Catholic practices in worship, e.g. there is a clear statement which says, *"Religious worship is to be given to God, the Father, Son and Holy Spirit and only to Him, not to angels, saints or any other creature. Since the Fall, this worship must involve a mediator and there is no other mediator than Christ alone."* (21:2) Concerning prayer the

Confession states, *"Prayer is to be made for lawful things and for people who are alive or may be born, but not for the dead, nor for those who are known to have committed the sin unto death."*(21:4)

(3)   Promises made to God

In a chapter entitled *"Concerning Lawful Oaths and Vows"* it is stated at the end of the chapter that, *"No one may vow to do anything forbidden in the word of God, anything hindering a duty commanded in the word, or anything not in his own power, which he has neither the ability nor warrant from God to perform. In this respect Roman Catholic monastic vows of perpetual celibacy, professed poverty and consistent obedience do not perfect us but are actually superstitious, sinful traps, in which no Christian should entangle himself."* (22:7)

(4)   The Christian and the State

In the chapter entitled, "Concerning Civil Authorities" it is stated that, *"The Pope of course, has no power and jurisdiction over civil authorities, or the people under them in secular affairs. The Pope never has any right to usurp secular authority, particularly capital punishment in cases of what is judged to be heresy or any other fault."* (23:4)

(5)   Marriage and Divorce

In this chapter it is stated that, *"Those who profess the reformed religion should not marry with infidels, Roman Catholics or other idolaters."*

(6)   Presbyterians and the Pope

In the chapter dealing with *"The Church"* we find what is probably regarded by Roman Catholics as the most notorious and repugnant statement of the *Confession* where it states; *"There is no other head of the Church than the Lord Jesus Christ. In no sense can the Pope in Rome be the head of it. Rather he is that Antichrist, the man of sin and son of damnation, who glorifies himself as opposed to Christ and everything else related to God."*

(7)   The Sacrament of the Lord's Supper

In a statement of how Presbyterians understand the Eucharist or what Roman Catholics call the Mass, in a section dealing with the once-for-all nature of Christ's atoning sacrifice on the Cross for the remission of our sins, it is stated that, *"the so-called sacrifice of the Roman Catholic Mass does detestable injustice to Christ's one sacrifice, which is the only propitiation for all the sins of the elect."* (29:2)

In 1988 the General Assembly of the Presbyterian Church (the supreme 'court' of the Church) in Ireland sought to clarify its understanding of the statement in the *Confession* identifying the Pope as the "Antichrist". The following resolution was passed:

In exercising the right to interpret and explain her standards the Church may set forth her understanding of the meaning of disputed passages. Chapter 25: paragraph 6 of the Westminster Confession of Faith steadfastly proclaims the Lord Jesus Christ as the only King and Head of the Church. From this it follows that no mere man can be head thereof, and that any claim to such headship is unbiblical. The General Assembly, under God, reaffirm this teaching but declare further to their understanding that the historical interpretation of the Pope of Rome as the personal and literal fulfilment of the Biblical figure of "the Antichrist" is not manifestly evident from the Scripture. A variety of views has long been held on this topic consistent with a loyal regard for the authority of Holy Scripture and a genuine acceptance of Reformation standards.

The Presbyterian Church in Ireland's Attitude to the Roman Catholic Church

In 1861 the General Assembly said "We recognise the Roman Catholic Church as a Church of Christ though in error". This remains the official position of the Church today.

In 1966 the General Assembly passed a resolution urging its members "humbly and frankly to acknowledge and to ask forgiveness for any attitudes and actions towards our Roman Catholic fellow-countrymen which have been unworthy of our calling as followers of Jesus Christ".

In 1990 a statement on "Agreements and Disagreements of Irish Presbyterianism and Roman Catholicism" was passed by the General Assembly after various drafts had been discussed by Kirk Sessions and Presbyteries (subordinate 'courts' of the Church). It speaks of *"Important areas of agreement on such fundamental doctrines as the Holy Trinity and the Divinity and Humanity of our Lord and his unique role in man's salvation"*. The document goes on to say *"Nevertheless there are basic disagreements between Presbyterians and Roman Catholics on the question of authority for Christian doctrine and practice and more specifically on their understanding of how men and women are saved by Jesus Christ"*. For Presbyterians, scripture alone is the authoritative source of Christian teaching and practice and salvation is by grace alone. The document's conclusion is that *"While rejoicing in those important things in which we are agreed we must acknowledge that our many differences remain irreconcilable within a single Church"* and that *"in spite of welcome changes in attitude towards 'separated brethren'…there appears to have been no fundamental change in Roman Catholic teaching and practice… While Presbyterians rejoice in the better relationships which are now experienced between Roman Catholics and Protestants in general, e.g. participation together in prayer and bible study, they do not see much evidence of the radical changes which would be necessary to make any significant reconciliation between our two Churches possible, but we must always remember that with God all things are possible."*

APPENDIX V

How the Methodist Church in Ireland Views the Roman Catholic Church

John Wesley was the founder of Methodism. Eric Gallagher in his pamphlet *A Better Way for Irish Protestants and Roman Catholics: Advice from John Wesley* says:
> *There are various remarks in his writings, perhaps best summed up in the reference in his "Notes on the New Testament" to the Pope as the "Man of Sin". And of course, again and again he has disparaging things to say about the Roman system which he summed up as Popery. For instance in 1785 he wrote to an Irish exile in the West Indies, John Stretton, "If that deadly enemy of true religion, Popery, is breaking in upon you, there is indeed no time to be lost"[1].*

But Wesley's attitude to Roman Catholics is best known from his letter to a Roman Catholic written in Dublin on 18 July 1748, "Whatever he had to say about the Church of Rome and its system, there is no doubt for him what personal relationships ought to be...We must respect each other as fellow Christians. We can, indeed must, on occasion disagree but our basic duty of Christian love remains."[2]

The 1960 Conference's View of the Church's Mission to Roman Catholic Ireland

This is the opinion expressed by the Methodist Conference shortly before Vatican II:

1. *That our witness to Roman Catholic Ireland should be regarded as part of our larger responsibility as Christians and members of the Church to spread the good news of Jesus Christ to all who do not know Him intimately as personal Lord and Saviour.*

2. *That since our peculiar responsibility for Roman Catholics in Ireland springs from the historic insights of the Reformation, our mission to Roman Catholics should be pursued with intimate knowledge and deep appreciation of their background and beliefs as well as of our own.*

3. *That the aim of our mission to Roman Catholics should be to lead them to saving faith in Jesus Christ as Saviour and Lord. Our approach should not be directly controversial, but rather with the humility of those who*

themselves are constantly exposed to the judgement of the living Word of God and yet convinced that an evangelical fellowship is necessary to full growth in Christian experience and service.[3]

Re-affirmation of Belief

The following resolution appears in the *Minutes of Conference,* 1966, shortly after Vatican II and expresses a cautiously more positive view:

The Conference hereby re-affirms its adherence to the declaration of the Church's belief as set out in the Manual of Laws, pages 13 and 14. It affirms in particular that its loyalty to the principles of the Protestant Reformation is not and has not been in question. It has willingly entered into conversations with other member Churches in Ireland of the World Council of Churches regarding the implications of the New Delhi statement of the World Council on the unity of the Church (Minutes of Conference, 1963, pp. 122-123). The Roman Catholic Church is not a member of the World Council and there has not at any time been any suggestion of "conversations" of this kind with that Church. The Conference calls upon our people to continue to pray for Roman Catholics and to pray and hope for a change in those beliefs which, we believe, it holds sincerely but in error. The Conference is mindful of John Wesley's wish that we should be the friends of all and the enemies of none.

The Conference welcomes the development of better understanding among all sections of the community in Ireland. It has considered the circumstances in which the Roman Catholic Priests were invited to address selected groups of our Ministers and People, and recognises that these invitations were issued in order to make those addressed more informed with regard to the Roman position on certain matters of concern to World Christendom and that such invitations implied no disloyalty to our Church or its teaching. It would welcome reciprocal invitations with a view to a clearer mutual understanding of Protestant and Roman Catholic positions on questions of social and religious concern, and is of the opinion that no objection can be properly taken to selected groups of our People listening to and questioning Roman Catholics on such issues.[4]

Inter-Church Activity

The following statement was adopted by the 1987 Conference:

It is important to understand what Inter-Church activity implies and what it does not. It does not imply that each participating Church accepts all that the others believe. It does not imply that they are actively attempting to "sink differences" and reach a "common denominator". It does imply that each accepts the sincerity and contribution of the others, that all believe that God has a purpose and will for His Church, that each is trying sincerely to discover and do that will, and that each denomination is part of the Body of Christ. In the context of a search for God's will for His Church, joint prayer, study and action to this end and for a better understanding of each other is to be positively encouraged.

In many parts of the country joint worship, prayer and study has become an established fact in relationships with Roman Catholics. This has been a learning and enriching experience for those involved, not least in helping Methodists to a deeper awareness of their own riches and tradition. The basis of sharing is the spirit and mind of Christ.

It is important to recognise that when Roman Catholics extend invitations to participate in joint activities, they most assuredly do not consider that we see everything as they do, nor do they suggest that they approve of all we believe. The issuing and acceptance of such invitations should be regarded as a declaration of a common recognition of the Christian tradition, in its several forms, as part of our Irish heritage. It should underline a common prayer that the people of this island should come to recognise the Salvation and Lordship of Christ and to know the mind and will of God.

Provided always that these facts are recognised, individuals should be free to exercise their Christian commitment with due regard to all the circumstances...

In obedience to Christ and to our Methodist tradition, to act together is a sign of the wholeness of Christ in a broken society. The ultimate loyalty for all Christians is loyalty to Christ and to the standards and values of His Kingdom. When expressed together there is a more effective witness to Christ's healing and reconciling love.[5]

References

(1) Eric Gallagher, *A Better Way for Irish Protestants and Roman Catholics: Advice from John Wesley* (Mission Board, Methodist Church in Ireland, Belfast, 1973), pp. 7-8.

(2) ibid., p.9 and p.12.

(3) Methodist Church in Ireland, *Minutes of Conference* (1960), p. 112.

(4) Methodist Church in Ireland, *Minutes of Conference* (1966), p. 131.

(5) Methodist Church in Ireland, *Minutes of Conference* (1987), pp. 53-54.

APPENDIX VI

How Evangelicals Regard the Roman Catholic Church

Many in the Christian Churches use the word 'evangelical'. It came into use at the reformation to identify Protestants. However, the people who we are discussing are a more restricted group – **conservative evangelicals**. The Evangelical Contribution on Northern Ireland group estimates that one-third of active Northern Ireland Protestants would consider themselves as 'evangelicals', and most of these would be conservative evangelicals.

The major emphases common to all conservative evangelicals would be the importance of personal conversion and the recognition of the full authority and complete inerrancy of the Holy Scriptures (Old and New Testaments). Conservative evangelicals would differ from fundamentalists in that they would have a healthy regard for Biblical scholarship, would seek to defend their view of Scripture on the basis of such scholarship and some may interpret inerrancy in a wider sense (e.g. authorial intent). It can be recognised from this that **truth**, particularly scriptural truth, is especially important to conservative evangelicals, and therefore 'error' is to be taken equally seriously.

Conservative evangelicals would find great difficulty in accepting certain Roman Catholic teachings which they would regard as having no foundation in Scripture, e.g. Baptismal Regeneration, The Immaculate Conception and Bodily Assumption of Mary, Prayers for the Dead, Prayers to the Saints and to Mary. The Roman Catholic Church is seen as being in serious 'error' on these issues.

From this common position various attitudes are taken by conservative evangelicals towards the Roman Catholic Church:

(1) **There are those who could not accept that a Church could hold so many apparently unscriptural teachings and still remain a Christian Church.** That, of course, does not mean that there are no Christians within it. In Northern Ireland many conservative evangelicals would find it difficult to accept the Roman Catholic Church as a Christian Church and this helps explain their refusal to be involved in joint acts of worship with Roman Catholics (particularly Roman Catholic clergy). They would see it as a compromise of the Gospel.

(2)   **Other conservative evangelicals would accept the official view of the Presbyterian Church in Ireland which states, "We recognise the Roman Catholic Church as a Church of Christ, yet in much error"**. Such acceptance would be on the basis of the many doctrines held in common and the recognition that the Catholic or Universal Church transcends all the denominational boundaries. However, in the context of Ireland, it would be only a minority of conservative evangelicals who would take this position. Holding to this view would enable some conservative evangelicals to engage in joint acts of worship that involve Roman Catholic clergy.

In both these groups some would be happy to have opportunity to meet with Roman Catholics to study the Bible, to discuss the Christian faith and to act together on issues of community concern. Some in so doing would make a distinction between recognising and cooperating with individual Roman Catholic *Christians* and recognising and cooperating with the Roman Catholic Church. There may also be a distinction between cooperating at an informal level and at an official Church level. Many conservative evangelicals have very real fears that other conservative evangelicals will accuse them of compromising the Gospel by meeting with Roman Catholics.

There is another group who might be better regarded as **fundamentalists**. They believe that it is necessary to separate from error and to purify the Church. They would believe that it is impossible in principle for Roman Catholics to be Christians and they would insist that if they become Christians they would have to validate that by leaving the Roman Catholic Church. Many Free Presbyterians would hold this view. Some fundamentalists (indeed, some conservative evangelicals) are politically orientated and others are firmly non-political.

The Free Presbyterian Church

Its dominant view of the Roman Catholic Church is that the **Pope is the Antichrist and that the Roman Catholic Church is the Beast spoken of in the book of the Revelation**. Such a view means that it finds it impossible to accept the Roman Catholic Church as in any way Christian and the Rev. Dr. Ian Paisley often makes the remark "No peace with Rome until Rome makes peace with God".

There is a strong separatist mentality in the Church which means that Free Presbyterians are almost as suspicious of the other Protestant Churches as they are of the Roman Catholic Church. They have also created their own separate school system. Dr. Paisley's background is Independent Baptist and he was never a Presbyterian. The adoption of the name 'Presbyterian' in the title of the Church was an attempt to lay claim to the main Presbyterian tradition and to say that the Presbyterian Church in Ireland had abandoned it through apostasy and error. The Free Presbyterian Church looks on itself as the true defender of the Protestant heritage.

While the Free Presbyterian Church contains only a small minority of the Protestant population (some 13,000) , the Democratic Unionist Party (which is dominated by members of the Church) has come to personify the political face of Ulster Protestant-ism (around one-third of the Protestant electorate regularly vote for it) . Support for the Party expresses the deep fears of many Ulster Protestants of losing the connection with Britain and being swallowed up in a united Ireland in which they feel the Roman Catholic Church would dominate and the Protestant heritage be lost.

Research Evidence

Research by Boal, Livingstone and Cámpbell[1] among Church-going Protestants in Belfast in the mid-1980s found that they could be divided into three groups: *liberals, liberal-conservative* and *fundamentalist*. These labels are not necessarily used in the way we have used them above. The definition of *fundamentalists* used by the authors is those who insist on the all-importance of a conversion experience and on a strictly inerrantist conception of the Bible. *Liberals* reject these two notions. The *liberal-conservatives* share many of the doctrinal and moral sympathies of the *fundamentalists* (notably on Church attendance, opposition to the World Council of Churches and in feelings about abortion) but hold a more liberal stance on integrated education, on politics and Sunday opening. The relative strength of the three groups was:

liberals	over 50%
liberal-conservatives	ca 20%
fundamentalists	ca 25%

Of the *fundamentalists* up to a third would have no dealings with the Roman Catholic Church whatsover and the rest were only prepared to have dealings on social issues. *Liberals* would have dealings with the Roman Catholic Church on both religious and social matters. But only one-third of **all** Church-going Protestants were prepared to worship with Roman Catholics.

Recent research by Inge Radford[2] shows that joint worship is the most problematic area for inter-church cooperation. Morrow found[3] that 5 per cent of Methodist clergy, 18 per cent of Church of Ireland clergy and 44 per cent of Presbyterian clergy would not participate in joint worship with Roman Catholics.

Boal, Livingstone and Campbell found that *fundamentalists* were more likely to vote for the Democratic Unionist Party; *liberals* to support the Official Unionist Party and the Alliance Party.

References

(1)   F. W. Boal, J. A. Campbell and D. N. Livingstone, "The Protestant Mosaic: A Majority of Minorities" in P. Roche and B. Barton (eds.), *The Northern Ireland Question : Myth and Reality* (Aldershot, 1991).

(2)   Inge Radford, *Breaking Down Divisions: The Possibility of a Local Church Contribution to Improving Community Relations* (Northern Ireland Community Relations Council, 1993).

(3)   Duncan Morrow, op.cit.

POLITICAL SOURCES

APPENDIX VII

The Anglo-Irish Agreement, November 1985
A Government Statement by The Northern Ireland Office:

TIME FOR TRUTH

Ever since the Anglo-Irish Agreement was signed on 15 November it has been the target of a sustained campaign of half-truths and worse. It is now time – for all our futures – to put the record straight.

It's an Agreement which guarantees Northern Ireland's position within the United Kingdom, as long as a majority here wants it. It's an Agreement which gives support for a devolved Government in Northern Ireland. It's an Agreement which is bringing increasing cross-border security cooperation. Developments which most people and politicians in Northern Ireland want. Yet the Agreement has been made the target of a deliberate campaign of lies, deceit, distortion and half-truths. A campaign exploiting emotions and leading to unrest and disorder, putting in danger jobs now and in the future.

It's time to sort out the facts from the daily diet of fictions. The fictions of those who before and since 15 November have said that the Agreement meant:

– the RUC would drop Royal from its name
– the UDR would be disbanded
– the style and colour of the RUC uniform would change
– Royal visits to Northern Ireland would have to have Southern approval

None of those claims was true, as everybody can now see. Nor are charges that:

Fiction: The Agreement represents 'Dublin Rule'.

FACT: The Irish Republic does *not* have 'joint authority' over any aspect of the affairs of Northern Ireland. The Agreement says 'there is no derogation from the sovereignty of either the United Kingdom Government or the Irish Government, and each retains responsibility for the decisions and administration of

Government within its own jurisdiction.' The Irish Government can express *views* and put forward *proposals*. But responsibility for the government of Northern Ireland remains firmly with British Ministers responsible to Parliament in London.

Fiction: Elected representatives in Northern Ireland are excluded and ignored.

FACT: The Prime Minister invited the Unionists to enter into discussions with her. The Secretary of State has repeatedly invited them to enter into discussions with him. The Unionists have refused all these offers; most of their MPs are also boycotting Parliament at Westminster. Unionist councillors are boycotting their councils in an attempt to wreck local government, and Unionist members of the Assembly are refusing to carry out the normal job of examining and influencing legislation and other matters affecting Northern Ireland.

Fiction: The Prime Minister has rejected or ignored the results of the 23 January by-elections.

FACT: The Prime Minister made clear that she respected the strength of unionist feeling. In response to it, she put forward proposals for talks on:

- new arrangements for Unionists to make their views known to the Government on the affairs of Northern Ireland;
- the future of the Northern Ireland Assembly;
- the arrangements for handling Northern Ireland's business in Parliament at Westminster.

She also agreed to consider positively the Unionist leaders' suggestion for a Round Table Conference, to discuss devolution in Northern Ireland.

Fiction: The Agreement will not help stop the violence.

FACT: Many of the Agreement's opponents said that the Irish Republic would never sign the European Convention on the Suppression of Terrorism, but it has. A prime aim of the Agreement is to increase cooperation between the UK and the Republic in the fight against terrorism and violence. This is something that both Governments are determined to achieve.

20 March 1986

APPENDIX VIII

1986
Two views of the Anglo-Irish Agreement:
By two party leaders: Ulster Unionist Party
and Democratic Unionist Party

A call to action by: Jim Molyneaux, M.P., and Ian Paisley, M.P.

A. 'A call to action'

The Anglo-Irish Agreement gives the Dublin Government a real say in Ulster's affairs while your own elected representatives are excluded and ignored.

Under Joint Authority Dublin's Minister for Northern Ireland, Peter Barry, has been set up over us as an equal with Tom King. Together they are intent on forcing Ulster down the Dublin Road.

The people of Ulster have rightly and emphatically said 'NO'. On 23rd January, 1986, 418,230 constitutionalists voted against the Agreement.

Yet at our meeting on 25th February the Prime Minister rejected the mandated and reasoned case which we presented on your behalf. By reaffirming her Government's commitment to the implementation of the Agreement she said 'NO' to the Ballot Box and spurned consultation in favour of confrontation.

It is now up to us all to demonstrate beyond doubt that we will not be trampled on in this manner and that in no circumstances will we ever accept Dublin Rule.

Next Monday is your opportunity to do so, by joining in a Massive Province-wide DAY OF ACTION AND PROTEST. We are asking you to play your part in sending an unmistakable signal to Westminster that Ulster means business.

B. 'Do you know?'

(1)   That under the Anglo-Irish Agreement Dublin's Minister, Peter Barry, presides as an equal with Tom King in a Conference which can deal with all the internal affairs of Northern Ireland.

(2)   That there is no recognition of the status of Northern Ireland as part of the U.K. in the Agreement. Dublin continues through its Constitution to claim the territory of Northern Ireland.

(3)   That following the powers given to it in respect of security the Dublin Government has boasted that it will be putting forward proposals to get rid of the U.D.R.

(4)   That Dublin can now jointly direct the Chief Constable of the R.U.C. Article 9(a) of the Agreement says, ' . . . the Conference shall set in hand a programme of work to be undertaken by the Chief Constable . . . '

(5)   That Dublin now has a right to make nominations for every public body in Northern Ireland, including the Police Authority and even the Education

and Health Boards. Furthermore these Dublin 'placemen' needn't even live in Northern Ireland.

(6) That 'Barry's Law' instead of 'British Law' will now operate in the banning of traditional loyalist parades. The Agreement gives Dublin the right to know about all planned parades and the opportunity to make its views known on them.

(7) That when Dublin makes proposals relating to any matters in N. Ireland the British Government is under a legally enforceable obligation to make 'determined efforts' to resolve any differences. Thus Her Majesty's Government is no longer free to govern Northern Ireland as it thinks fit. Dublin will call the tune and the N.I.O. will scrape and bow to win the Republic's approval. A DUBLIN ROLE IS DUBLIN RULE.

(8) That under the Agreement Dublin is insisting on the repeal of the Flags and Emblems Act so that the Irish Tricolour can freely fly anywhere in Northern Ireland.

(9) That the Agreement heralds the establishment of 'MIXED COURTS' in which judges from the Republic would sit in Northern Ireland Courts.

(10) The S.D.L.P. has now an absolute veto on all possible devolution in Northern Ireland. Even with devolution the Conference would continue with its powers undiluted over security, the Courts, human rights and all other vital matters.

Little wonder Ulster emphatically voted against this obnoxious Agreement on 23rd January. This Agreement is the blueprint for an All-Ireland and as such must meet with unrelenting opposition from every Unionist. It cannot be reformed; it must be destroyed.

The Unionist leadership is pledged in solidarity to achieve this end. With your help it can be done!

Issued by the Unionist Joint Working Party, Parliament Buildings, Stormont.

APPENDIX IX

Joint Declaration

The following is the text of the Joint Declaration by the Prime Minister, Rt. Hon. John Major, MP, and the Taoiseach, Mr Albert Reynolds, TD, on the 15th December 1993.

(1)   The Taoiseach, Mr Albert Reynolds, TD, and the Prime Minister, the Rt. Hon. John Major, MP, acknowledge that the most urgent and important issue facing the people of Ireland, North and South, and the British and Irish Governments together, is to remove the causes of conflict, to overcome the legacy of history and to heal the divisions which have resulted, recognising that the absence of a lasting and satisfactory settlement of relationships between the peoples of both islands has contributed to continuing tragedy and suffering. They believe that the development of an agreed framework for peace, which has been discussed between them since early last year, and which is based on a number of key principles articulated by the two Governments over the past 20 years, together with the adaptation of other widely accepted principles, provides the starting point of a peace process designed to culminate in a political settlement.

(2)   The Taoiseach and the Prime Minister are convinced of the inestimable value to both their peoples, and particularly for the next generation, of healing divisions in Ireland and of ending a conflict which has been so manifestly to the detriment of all. Both recognise that the ending of divisions can come about only through the agreement and cooperation of the people, North and South, representing both traditions in Ireland. They therefore make a solemn commitment to promote cooperation at all levels on the basis of the fundamental principles, undertakings, obligations under international agreements, to which they have jointly committed themselves, and the guarantees which each Government has given and now reaffirms, including Northern Ireland's statutory constitutional guarantee. It is their aim to foster agreement and reconciliation, leading to a new political framework founded on consent and encompassing arrangements within Northern Ireland, for the whole island, and between these islands.

(3)   They also consider that the development of Europe will, of itself, require new approaches to serve interests common to both parts of the island of Ireland, and to Ireland and the United Kingdom as partners in the European Union.

(4)   The Prime Minister, on behalf of the British Government, reaffirms that they will uphold the democratic wish of a greater number of the people of Northern Ireland on the issue of whether they prefer to support the Union or a

sovereign united Ireland. On this basis, he reiterates, on behalf of the British Government, that they have no selfish strategic or economic interest in Northern Ireland. Their primary interest is to see peace, stability and reconciliation established by agreement among all the people who inhabit the island, and they will work together with the Irish Government to achieve such an agreement, which will embrace the totality of relationships. The role of the British Government will be to encourage, facilitate and enable the achievement of such agreement over a period through a process of dialogue and cooperation based on full respect for the rights and identities of both traditions in Ireland. They accept that such agreement may, as of right, take the form of agreed structures for the island as a whole, including a united Ireland achieved by peaceful means on the following basis. The British Government agree that it is for the people of the island of Ireland alone, by agreement between the two parts respectively, to exercise their right of self-determination on the basis of consent, freely and concurrently given, North and South, to bring about a united Ireland, if that is their wish. They reaffirm as a binding obligation that they will, for their part, introduce the necessary legislation to give effect to this, or equally to any measure of agreement on future relationships in Ireland which the people living in Ireland may themselves freely so determine without external impediment. They believe that the people of Britain would wish, in friendship to all sides, to enable the people of Ireland to reach agreement on how they may live together in harmony and in partnership, with respect for their diverse traditions, and with full recognition of the special links and the unique relationship which exist between the peoples of Britain and Ireland.

(5) The Taoiseach, on behalf of the Irish Government, considers that the lessons of Irish history, and especially of Northern Ireland, show that stability and well-being will not be found under any political system which is refused allegiance or rejected on grounds of identity by a significant minority of those governed by it. For this reason, it would be wrong to attempt to impose a united Ireland, in the absence of the freely given consent of a majority of the people of Northern Ireland. He accepts, on behalf of the Irish Government, that the democratic right of self-determination by the people of Ireland as a whole must be achieved and exercised with and subject to the agreement and consent of a majority of the people of Northern Ireland and must, consistent with justice and equity, respect the democratic dignity and civil rights and religious liberties of both communities, including:

– the right of free political thought;
– the right to freedom and expression of religion;
– the right to pursue democratically national and political aspirations;
– the right to seek constitutional change by peaceful and legitimate means;
– the right to live wherever one chooses without hindrance;
– the right to equal opportunity in all social and economic activity, regardless of class, creed, sex or colour.

These would be reflected in any future political and constitutional arrangements emerging from a new and more broadly based agreement.

(6)   The Taoiseach however recognises the genuine difficulties and barriers to building relationships of trust either within or beyond Northern Ireland, from which both traditions suffer. He will work to create a new era of trust, in which suspicion of the motives or actions of others is removed on the part of either community. He considers that the future of the island depends on the nature of the relationship between the two main traditions that inhabit it. Every effort must be made to build a new sense of trust between those communities. In recognition of the fears of the Unionist community and as a token of his willingness to make a personal contribution to the building up of that necessary trust, the Taoiseach will examine with his colleagues any elements in the democratic life and organisation of the Irish State that can be represented to the Irish Government in the course of political dialogue as a real and substantial threat to their way of life and ethos, or that can be represented as not being fully consistent with a modern democratic and pluralist society, and undertakes to examine any possible ways of removing such obstacles. Such an examination would of course have due regard to the desire to preserve those inherited values that are largely shared throughout the island or that belong to the cultural and historical roots of the people of this island in all their diversity. The Taoiseach hopes that over time a meeting of hearts and minds will develop, which will bring all the people of Ireland together, and will work towards that objective, but he pledges in the meantime that as a result of the efforts that will be made to build mutual confidence no Northern Unionist should ever have to fear in future that this ideal will be pursued either by threat or coercion.

(7)   Both Governments accept that Irish unity would be achieved only by those who favour this outcome persuading those who do not, peacefully and without coercion or violence, and that, if in future a majority of the people of Northern Ireland are so persuaded, both Governments will support and give legislative effect to their wish. But, notwithstanding the solemn affirmation by both Governments in the Anglo-Irish Agreement that any change in the status of Northern Ireland would only come about with the consent of a majority of the people of Northern Ireland, the Taoiseach also recognises the continuing uncertainties and misgivings which dominate so much of Northern Unionist attitudes towards the rest of Ireland. He believes that we stand at a stage of our history when the genuine feelings of all traditions in the North must be recognised and acknowledged. He appeals to both traditions at this time to grasp the opportunity for a fresh start and a new beginning, which could hold such promise for all our lives and the generations to come. He asks the people of Northern Ireland to look on the people of the Republic as friends, who share their grief and shame over all the suffering of the last quarter of a century and who want to develop the best possible relationship with them, a relationship in which trust and new understanding can flourish and grow. The Taoiseach also acknowledges the presence in the Constitution of the Republic of elements which are deeply resented by Northern unionists, but which, at the same time, reflect

hopes and ideals which lie deep in the hearts of many Irish men and women North and South. But as we move towards a new era of understanding in which new relationships of trust may grow and bring peace to the island of Ireland, the Taoiseach believes that the time has come to consider together how best the hopes and identities of all can be expressed in more balanced ways, which no longer engender division and the lack of trust to which he has referred. He confirms that, in the event of an overall settlement, the Irish Government will, as part of a balanced constitutional accommodation, put forward and support proposals for change in the Irish Constitution which would fully reflect the principle of consent in Northern Ireland.

(8) The Taoiseach recognises the need to engage in dialogue which would address with honesty and integrity the fears of all traditions. But that dialogue, both within the North and between the people and their representatives of both parts of Ireland, must be entered into with an acknowledgement that the future security and welfare of the people of the island will depend on an open, frank and balanced approach to all the problems which for too long have caused division.

(9) The British and Irish Governments will seek, along with the Northern Ireland constitutional parties through a process of political dialogue, to create institutions and structures which, while respecting the diversity of the people of Ireland, would enable them to work together in all areas of common interest. This will help over a period to build the trust necessary to end past divisions, leading to an agreed and peaceful future. Such structures would, of course, include institutional recognition of the special links that exist between the peoples of Britain and Ireland as part of the totality of relationships, while taking account of newly forged links with the rest of Europe.

(10) The British and Irish Governments reiterate that the achievement of peace must involve a permanent end to the use of, or support for, paramilitary violence. They confirm that, in these circumstances, democratically mandated parties which establish a commitment to exclusively peaceful methods and which have shown that they abide by the democratic process, are free to participate fully in democratic politics and to join in dialogue in due course between the Governments and the political parties on the way ahead.

(11) The Irish Government would make their own arrangements within their jurisdiction to enable democratic parties to consult together and share in dialogue about the political future. The Taoiseach's intention is that these arrangements could include the establishment, in consultation with other parties, of a Forum for Peace and Reconciliation to make recommendations on ways in which agreement and trust between both traditions in Ireland can be promoted and established.

(12) The Taoiseach and the Prime Minister are determined to build on the fervent wish of both their peoples to see old fears and animosities replaced

by a climate of peace. They believe the framework they have set out offers the people of Ireland, North and South, whatever their tradition, the basis to agree that from now on their differences can be negotiated and resolved exclusively by peaceful political means. They appeal to all concerned to grasp the opportunity for a new departure. That step would compromise no position or principle, nor prejudice the future for either community. On the contrary, it would be an incomparable gain for all. It would break decisively the cycle of violence and the intolerable suffering it entails for the people of these islands, particularly for both communities in Northern Ireland. It would allow the process of economic and social cooperation on the island to realise its full potential for prosperity and mutual understanding. It would transform the prospects for building on the progress already made in the Talks process, involving the two Governments and the constitutional parties in Northern Ireland. The Taoiseach and the Prime Minister believe that these arrangements offer an opportunity to lay the foundations for a more peaceful and harmonious future devoid of the violence and bitter divisions which have scarred the past generation. They commit themselves and their Governments to continue to work together, unremittingly, towards that objective.

15 December 1993

APPENDIX X

Frameworks for the Future: a Summary

Part I – 'A Framework for Accountable Government in Northern Ireland' – is a paper by the British Government. It offers proposals for possible new democratic institutions in Northern Ireland.

Part II – 'A New Framework for Agreement' – is a joint paper by the British and Irish Governments, which has come to be known as the Joint Framework Document. It offers proposals for relationships within the island of Ireland, and between the two Governments.

Neither paper is put forward as a blueprint, to be imposed. The proposals in each are offered for further discussion in the Talks process. Part I is offered as an aid to negotiation involving the Northern Ireland parties and the British Government. Part II serves the same purpose for negotiation involving the Northern Ireland parties and the British and Irish Governments.

A Framework for Accountable Government in Northern Ireland

These proposals:

- outline the British Government's understanding of where agreement might be found amongst the political parties and the wider community on new democratic institutions within Northern Ireland;

- identify the characteristics that should underlie any such new institutions;

- propose and describe in greater detail:

  - a single unicameral Assembly of about 90 members elected for a fixed term;

  - legislative and executive responsibility over as wide a range of subjects as in 1973;

  - elections to the Assembly by a form of proportional representation;

  - possibly a separate Panel, perhaps of 3 people elected within Northern Ireland, to complement the working of the Assembly;

  - a system of Assembly Committees, constituted broadly in proportion to party strengths in the Assembly;

  - a system of detailed checks and balances intended to sustain confidence in the institutions.

A New Framework for Agreement

These proposals:

- reaffirm the guiding principles of self-determination, the consent of the governed, exclusively democratic and peaceful means, and full respect and protection for the rights and identities of both traditions;

- provide for an agreed new approach to traditional constitutional doctrines on both sides:

  - the British Government will propose changes to its constitutional legislation, so as to incorporate a commitment to continuing willingness to accept the will of a majority of the people living in Northern Ireland, and a commitment to exercise their jurisdiction with rigorous impartiality on behalf of all the people of Northern Ireland, in a way which does not prejudice their freedom to determine Northern Ireland's constitutional status, whether in remaining a part of the United Kingdom or in forming part of a united Ireland;

  - the Irish Government will introduce and support proposals for changes in the Irish Constitution, so that no territorial claim of right to jurisdiction over Northern Ireland contrary to the will of a majority of its people is asserted, and so that the Irish Government recognise the legitimacy of whatever choice is freely exercised by a majority of the people of Northern Ireland with regard to its constitutional status;

- commend direct dialogue with the relevant political parties in Northern Ireland in developing new internal structures;

- propose a North/South body, comprising elected representatives from, and accountable to, a Northern Ireland Assembly and the Irish Parliament, to deal with matters designated by the two Governments in the first instance in agreement with the parties;

- describe ways in which such a body could work with executive, harmonising or consultative functions, by way of authority delegated to its members by the Assembly;

- envisage that all decisions within the North/South body would be by agreement between the two sides;

- set out criteria for the designation of functions, and suggest a range of functions that might be designated from the outset, for agreement with the parties;

- envisage the Northern Ireland Assembly and the Irish Parliament being able, by agreement, to designate further functions or to move functions already designated between the three categories;

- envisage that the body will have an important role, in consultation with the two Governments, in developing an agreed approach for the whole island in respect of the challenges and opportunities of the European Union;

- envisage a Parliamentary forum, with representatives from new Northern Ireland institutions and the Irish Parliament, to consider matters of mutual interest;

- envisage a new and more broadly based Agreement between the British and Irish Governments to develop and extend co-operation;

- envisage a standing Intergovernmental Conference which would consider matters of mutual interest, but not those transferred to new political institutions in Northern Ireland;

- envisage that representatives of agreed political institutions in Northern Ireland may be formally associated with the work of the Conference;

- provide for a complematary undertaking by both Governments to ensure protection for specified civil, political, social and cultural rights.

These proposals do *not* provide for joint authority by the British and Irish Governments over Northern Ireland; They do *not* predetermine any outcome to the Talks process. Agreement by the parties, and then by the people, is the key.

Copies of the full text of both documents for discussion are available at your main post office or by calling **Freefone No: 0800 374 964.**

22 February 1995

Index